0413 582701 1002

D0260175

Books should be
Books (not already
application, by writi...

Date Due
2 4 JUL 1990
2 7 OCT 1992
8 JAN

SANTRY BOOKSTORE
DUBLIN CORPORATION PUBLIC LIBRARIES

Borrow...

Damage t...

Borrower...

Fines ch...

A Video Arts Guide

So you think you're in business?

Video Arts

Cartoons by Shaun Williams

So you think you're in business?

Methuen . London

First published in Great Britain 1986
by Methuen London Ltd
11 New Fetter Lane, London EC4P 4EE
© 1986 Video Arts Ltd
Illustrations © 1986 Methuen London Ltd
Printed in Great Britain

British Library Cataloguing in Publication Data

So you think you're in business?—(A Video
    Arts guide)
    1. Business enterprises—Finance
    I. Video Arts   II. Series
    658.1′5   HG4026

    ISBN 0–413–58260–4
    ISBN 0–413–58270–1 Pbk

This title is available in both hardback and
paperback editions. The paperback is sold
subject to the condition that it shall not, by way
of trade or otherwise, be lent, re-sold, hired
out, or otherwise circulated without the
publisher's prior consent in any form of
binding or cover other than that in which it is
published and without a similar condition
including this condition being imposed on the
subsequent purchaser.

Video Arts Ltd can be contacted at
Dumbarton House,
68 Oxford Street,
London W1N 9LA

LEABHARLANNA ATHA CLIATH
DUBLIN MOBILE LIBRARIES
ACC. NO.   0413 582701
COPY NO.   1002
INV NO/89 3007
PRICE IR£   5.56
CLASS   658.15

Contents

A Video Arts Guide

So you think you're in business?

Ah, accounts . . . time to put on
my imbecile's hat . . .

You are a literate and intelligent person. You're no Einstein, but you can manage costings and budgets quite satisfactorily.

There is, however, one area that you do not seem able to get to grips with: the whole grey and foggy world of accountancy conventions and financial mumbo-jumbo, the world of balance sheets, capital and revenue transactions, working capital and the like. You feel slightly guilty about this, because you know it lies at the heart of every business. You also feel slightly resentful because, deep down, you have a suspicion that it isn't really all that complicated. It's just that no one has ever explained it to you in simple language, without all the accountants' jargon. You are quite right. It is indeed basically very simple. But some very sophisticated people come unstuck because they do not really understand how it all works.

So let's meet one of them. His name is Carruthers. He is very sophisticated, very grand, but extremely hazy about accountants' jargon. So to get a little help he consults the low-born, crude, but highly successful Ronald Scroggs.

Carruthers: My name is Julian Carruthers. I am deputy long-range planning executive of Universal International. We have companies all over the world. We turn over £700,000 million a year. Or is it £700 million? Or dollars? Anyway, something like that.

Scroggs: I am Ron Scroggs of Scroggs Manufacturing. I have a wooden shed in Brixton. Last year I turned over £46,328.53.

Carruthers: I work on the 51st floor of Universal House, and I am widely respected throughout the corporation.

Scroggs: I work in the corner of the shed,

1 The balance sheet barrier

9

and the lads think I'm a bastard.

Carruthers: I am a highly sophisticated
manager. I know all about the
Hawthorne Experiment, Theory X
and Theory Y, Hygiene Factors,
Blake's Grid and the Hierarchy of
Needs. The only thing I do not
understand is finance.

Scroggs: I am a highly unsophisticated
manager. I don't know what the hell
he's talking about. But I watch the
figures like a hawk.

Carruthers: My colleagues are all highly
sophisticated managers too. They do
not understand finance either. All of
us feel slightly uneasy about admitting
it, so we have a gentleman's
agreement not to refer to it. We leave
the financial arrangements to the
accounting people, just as we leave
the catering arrangements to the
canteen people. We believe in
trusting people.

Scroggs: I do not trust anybody, but then
fortunately I am not a gentleman. I
cut my own sandwiches and I do my
own accounts.

Carruthers: I would lose face if I
admitted to anyone in the corporation
that I do not understand finance,
since I am constantly approving
financial statements, draft accounts
and balance sheets.

Scroggs: If I did not understand finance I
would not lose face. But I would lose
all my money.

Carruthers: I have come to this man for
help because he is so crude and
ignorant that he will use short simple
words that I can understand; and not
the obscure mumbo-jumbo that
accountants try to frighten you with.

Scroggs: Because I am crude and
ignorant I am flattered by his

attention. But just what is it he does not understand?

Carruthers: Let me say first that I understand a great deal on a wide range of management subjects. The only thing I do not understand is how business actually works.

Do you know anyone like Carruthers? Many managers, even highly titled ones, share some of his characteristics, which mean two things. First, although they know a lot of *words*, they never quite know what they are doing when taking decisions about their business, with its interrelated profit and loss accounts, cash flow forecasts and revenue. Second, one day, they will make a catastrophic error – like accepting a profitable order which sends them bankrupt (yes, you can be profitable and bankrupt); or perhaps failing to seize a business opportunity because the accountants tell them it is loss-making (yes, loss-making companies can be turned round if you understand the business elements behind the losses and can see what to do about them).

Among the many things Carruthers does not understand is the basic description of a company presented by a balance sheet.

Scroggs: Right, we will start by looking at a balance sheet. It is the window which reveals the business.

Carruthers: It is not the window which reveals the business. It is the blind drawn by the accountants to keep the managers in the dark.

Scroggs: OK, if you prefer it then we will just talk about money. In business, money only does two things. It comes in, and it goes out. There are two basic things you have to know: 'where

did it come from?' and 'where did it go out to?' All right?

Carruthers: Yes, yes. I understand that.

Scroggs: So let's begin with where it comes from. Say you're starting a business. There's only two places you can get money from. The first is by risking your own, and perhaps getting some other people to share the risk with you. That money is called **share capital** or the **equity**, and the shareholders are the owners of the business and share all its profits. Or lose all their money. The second place you can get money from is someone else. You borrow it, on a long-term basis, and pay interest. That's called **loan capital**.

Carruthers: Light is beginning to dawn. There are only two places money can come from: share capital and loan capital. The owners' money and the money they borrow from someone else.

Scroggs: You've got it. Now you've raised the money. Where are you going to put it?

Carruthers: I am going to put it . . . into the business.

Scroggs: What part of the business?

Carruthers: Ah, the part of the business that . . . you tell me to.

Scroggs: Right. Well, just as there are only two places money can come from, there are only two places money can go out to. First, you can put it into things you mean to keep: buildings, machinery, cars, furniture. All those are called **fixed assets**. And second, you can put it into things you mean to sell: raw materials, piece-parts, packaging materials and so on. That money is called **working capital**.

Share capital

The chief characteristics of share capital are:

1 No interest has to be paid on shares, and the shareholders have no legal entitlement to any return on their investment. Instead, they own what is left (if anything) each year after the payment of all debts, costs and taxes, and can decide whether to put it back into the business (reserves) or divide it up amongst the shareholders in proportion to their shareholdings (dividends).

2 A shareholder has no right to take his money out of the business. All he can do is sell his shares, and if he cannot find anyone to buy them, that's just too bad.

3 The shares do not have a fixed value. They are worth what people will pay for them.

4 The share capital does not ever have to be returned and if the company is wound up, the shareholders get nothing until every other debt has been paid in full.

13

Loan capital

The chief characteristics of loan capital are:

1 The interest is a legal charge on the company which has to be paid when it is due, just like the rent. What is more, you have to pay the interest on the total sum lent for the whole period of the loan.

2 There is a date on which the lender is entitled to have his money back and you are legally bound to return it to him, unless of course he agrees to extend the terms of the loan.

3 The loan is repayable at its original value. If you borrowed £10,000 that is what you repay, irrespective of the rise or fall in the value of the company (or of money).

4 The return of the loan at the end of its term is a legal charge on the company. If the company is wound up, the proceeds go to repay secured loans before giving back to the shareholders any of their original capital.

Carruthers: Ah, I've heard of that.

So there is the basis of every business: the two places money can come from – **share capital**, risking your own, and **loan capital**, borrowing someone else's – and the two places it can go to: **fixed assets**, things you mean to keep, and **working capital**, things you mean to sell. It's extremely simple, and in fact the reason why balance sheets balance. All the money in a business on one side of the sheet, however described, is accounted for exactly on the other side of the sheet. It is not, however, the sum total of the knowledge you need to understand a balance sheet, let alone a business. If something is deceptively simple you can be certain Carruthers will be deceived . . .

Carruthers: I now know, which I knew all along but did not know that I knew, that a business is based on cash and that you start by saying where you got it and what you did with it. I now understand how a business works.

Scroggs: You do not understand how a business works because you do not understand working capital.

Carruthers: I cannot imagine why you think I do not understand working capital.

Scroggs: Then tell me, do you want a lot of money in working capital, or a little?

Carruthers: All capital is good, so I want a lot.

Scroggs: You want as little money as possible tied up in working capital.

Carruthers: I can now imagine why you think I do not understand working capital.

Fixed assets are the things you mean to keep.

Calculating
working capital

If your working capital keeps
moving all the time, how do you
ever know how much you actually
have at any given moment? How
do you know how much to enter in
the balance sheet under 'working
capital'? Well, first you shout
'stop!' You freeze everything at
5.30 pm on Friday and then you
simply count up what you've got.
On the balance sheet it would look
like:

WORKING CAPITAL

Current assets

Raw material	£50
Work in progress	£140
Finished goods	£90
Cash in hand	£150
Cash at bank	£240
Debtors	£150
	£820

Suppose you have just started a business.
You are going to manufacture cheap metal
teaspoons for the catering trade. You rent a
building at the bottom of the garden which
will serve as a factory workshop. Your own
sitting-room will serve as the office. You put
your savings into buying a Super Spoonmaster Fine Blanking Machine, a Master
Cutler Spoon Press and a set of teaspoon
pressing dies to go with it. Those are all
the fixed assets you need. You are fully
equipped. So off you go. But you don't.

You don't go because you haven't got
anyone to operate the Blanking Machine or
the Press, you haven't got any metal to make
the spoons with, you haven't insured the
building or the machines, you have no
lubricant and you have no telephone to call
hotels and restaurants to see whether they
need any teaspoons. You will also need
electricity to run the machines and heat the
workshop, and money for rent, rates, water,
paper, postage and advertising.

Of course, all this will be paid for by the
money your customers pay you for the
teaspoons, once you get going. But you work
out that you will need to spend £1000 on
labour, materials and overheads before the
money starts to come back. So you borrow it
from the bank (if you don't raise it from
shareholders) and start up. You have then invested a further £1000 in **working capital**.
Let Scroggs explain how working capital
works:

Scroggs: You need working capital to
keep you going. Then you can start
to make money.
Carruthers: How?
Scroggs: Look at Scroggs Manufacturing.
I make teaspoons. All I do is spend

£30 on ten kilos of light alloy strip on Monday, change its shape, and sell it for £150 on Friday. I buy another ten kilos of light alloy strip. I pay the lads. I pay the overheads. I put a bit aside. And I keep a bit for myself. Right?

Carruthers: No, I'm not happy.

Scroggs: Why not?

Carruthers: It's so simple I am getting suspicious.

Scroggs: Well, let's look a bit closer. Take that light alloy strip I buy on Monday for £30. On Tuesday I pay Harry £10 for stamping it into blanks. Now I've got £40 invested in stamped blanks. On Wednesday I pay George £10 to press blanks into spoons. Now I've got £50 invested in pressed spoons. On Thursday I pay Bill £10 to pack the spoons and take them to the collection bay. Now I've got £60 invested in packed spoons. On Friday I pay all the bills for the week's overheads. They come to £50. So now I've got £110 invested in a crate of teaspoons. That £110 is tied up in working capital. And so on Friday afternoon the customer collects the spoons and pays £150 for them. So I have recovered my investment of £110 in working capital and made £40 profit.

Carruthers: I see. You put in cash and get raw material. You put in more cash and get the raw material processed. You put in more cash to pay overheads. Then you sell something and get your working capital back with a bit over. It's really a sort of cash merry-go-round.

Scroggs: For a sophisticated manager that's quite a sensible statement.

Carruthers: Ah! I've got something right.

But you can't call all that your working capital – you put an advertisement in *Catering Hardware Monthly* last month and you haven't paid the bill yet. It cost £30. And you're off on your holidays at the weekend, so you'll be taking £140 of your profits off with you this evening. Those have to be subtracted. So after current assets we put:

Less **current liabilities**

Creditors	£30
Proposed dividend	£140
	£170

So – **net working capital**

(current assets less current liabilities)	£650

But always remember that the business itself is never static. It's always moving. If you'd shouted 'stop' five minutes earlier, it would all look quite different again. A balance sheet is a snapshot, freezing at one moment of time a perpetually moving and changing process.

I now understand working capital.
Sort of. I see that working capital is
all the money tied up in things that
you hope one day to sell to
customers. But I do not see how you
can live on £40 a week.

Scroggs: I do not have to live on £40 a
week.

Carruthers: Ah. You have a private
income.

Scroggs: I do not have a private income.
What has not struck you is that I
have a five-day week. I do not buy
light alloy strip on Mondays only – I
buy it every day. So every day Harry
stamps out ten kilos of blanks. Every
day George presses ten kilos of
spoons. Every day Bill packs the
spoons and takes them to the
collection bay. Every day a customer
collects the spoons and pays for them
– it is a continuous process all
through the year. So the cash
merry-go-round goes on all the time.
Tell me, how much do I clear a
week?

Carruthers: This is the sort of problem I
am good at, because I am
sophisticated. You clear £40 a day
five days a week. So you clear £200 a
week.

Carruthers may be sophisticated, but he has
walked straight into Scroggs's trap.

Scroggs: OK. If I spend £30 a day on
strip metal, how much do I spend a
week?

Carruthers: £150.

Scroggs: If I pay Harry £10 a day for
blanking, what do I pay him a week?

Carruthers: £50.

Scroggs: And George for pressing?
Carruthers: £50.
Scroggs: And Bill for packing?
Carruthers: £50.
Scroggs: Overheads?
Carruthers: £50.
Scroggs: So how much goes out every week?
Carruthers: £350.
Scroggs: And if I collect £150 on Monday, Tuesday, Wednesday, Thursday and Friday, how much do I collect a week?
Carruthers: Five times 150 is, er, £750.
Scroggs: So if I collect £750 a week, and spend £350 a week, how much do I clear?
Carruthers: Well . . . I said you cleared £200 a week, but you have proved that you clear £400 a week. I do not see how you have done this, but I do see how you can live on £400 a week.

Carruthers fell into the trap because he does not understand about **overheads**. Scroggs has to pay £50 a week overheads whether he makes one consignment of teaspoons or five consignments.Carruthers charged a week's overheads on every day's consignment, so he put four times £50 too much on to the costs. But you only pay a week's overheads once a week – overheads don't multiply like materials and labour – so the more consignments you produce each week, the more profit you make on each consignment, because they divide the overheads up into smaller shares. So on the cash merry-go-round it's only the first consignment of the week that costs £110. All the rest cost £60.

If you want to understand your business there are three groups of questions to which you must be able to find answers, and there is a special document designed to give the

I've always thought 'overheads' meant
the bits one couldn't understand . . .

answers to each group of questions.

So far we have looked at only one of these documents, the **balance sheet**. The balance sheet gives you a picture of the business at a single instant of time. But you will also want to be able to answer a group of questions about the past. Where did the money come from in the past? What was it spent on? Did I make a profit or loss – or to put it more accurately, did my money grow or shrink over the last twelve months? These questions are answered by the **profit and loss account**. The profit and loss account is, in effect, your history book.

Scroggs: Look at my profit and loss account for one week, starting with my income. I sold five lots of teaspoons at £150 a time. That brought in £750. I also got in £10 interest on some cash I put on deposit. Income £760. Now look at my expenses. I bought five lots of strip metal at £30 a time, so £150 went out on materials. I paid Harry and George £50 each, so £100 went out on manufacturing labour. I paid Bill £50, so £50 went out on distribution labour. I paid out £50 overheads and another £10 on bank interest. So I made a net profit of £400.

Carruthers: I now understand the profit and loss account. What I do not understand is this: if you are making £400 a week profit, why are you not filthy rich?

Scroggs: You do not understand why I am not filthy rich because you do not understand what profit is.

Carruthers: I understand perfectly well what profit is. Profit is champagne and cigars and a decent tailor.

Profit and loss

A profit and loss account is really simple. Every housewife runs her own profit and loss account with every week's housekeeping. And that's the trouble . . . the profit and loss account is hiding an awful lot from you. There are an awful lot of questions it isn't answering. It isn't telling you how your costs relate to your sales, for example. And suppose you've been making tablespoons as well as teaspoons – the profit and loss account may be concealing the fact that you're making a loss on all your tablespoon sales and a very big profit on all your teaspoon sales. You can find out, but you will have to ask for separate costings for each product. The profit and loss account is silent about the relative profitability of different lines; about how much capital is invested in the business; about whether the business is solvent (you might have made a profit of £50,000 last year and still be in the red).

Anyone can understand what a profit and loss account is telling them. What distinguishes the people who understand business from those who don't is that they understand what the profit and loss account *isn't* telling them.

Why make a profit?

Why do you have to make a profit? Why can't you just break even? Well, you may need to increase your fixed assets, buy another machine perhaps. If you're not making any profit, if every penny that comes in has to go straight out again to pay bills, you won't be able to.

You may want to replace the Super Spoonmaster because it's worn out. And you may have set aside each year, for five years, one-fifth of its cost. You bought it for £5000, you depreciated it by £1000 a year, and you invested that £1000 ready for replacement. But what's happened? Inflation over five years, and technological advance, have raised the price of the latest (Mark II) Super Spoonmaster to £8,500. Where are you going to find the extra £3,500, if not out of profit?

In other words, expanding the business in any way, and even merely keeping it up-to-date technically, requires profit.

Profit is not champagne and cigars and a decent tailor. Champagne and cigars and tailors are to do with cash. You can get cash from winning the pools, robbing banks or inheriting your rich uncle's fortune. Or from wages, salaries, interest, dividends or sale of shares. Dividends come out of profits; but there is no necessity to pay a dividend. If you do pay one you will pay it in cash, and the cash will pay for the cigars and champagne and tailors.

Profit is what lets the business grow. Working capital makes the business go round but it can't make it grow bigger – not unless it makes profit first. Suppose Scroggs wants to make his exports grow. He sends catalogues to a lot of Europe's teaspoon buyers. He needs extra money. Then, supposing he gets an export order every week, he has to produce an extra consignment – say another ten kilos of strip metal. More money is needed, for overtime, a new machine to help cope with the extra volume and so on.

There's no doubt about the best place to get extra money: use the extra that came out of the working capital money-go-round last year – in other words the **profit**. The first thing that happens to profit is that the taxman takes his slice of corporation tax. Then the directors and shareholders decide how much of what is left is needed to put back into the business for next year's development and growth. And the remainder, if any, is shared out as dividends. These *can* be spent on champagne and cigars – after paying income tax on those dividends. Scroggs amplifies the point.

Merely keeping a business up to date technically requires profit.

Scroggs: Remember the two places
money came from. Our own money
we risked, and the money we
borrowed?

Carruthers: Yes.

Scroggs: Once the business makes a
profit there's a third source – the
profit we put back into the business.
It's called **reserves**.

Carruthers: I understand reserves –
chests full of money stashed away in
a bank vault.

Scroggs: Reserves are not necessarily
stashed away in a vault. They could
be represented by machinery, or raw
materials or property.

Carruthers: Machinery can't be reserves.

Scroggs: Yes it can.

Carruthers: Well, you're using the word
in a very silly and misleading way.

Scroggs: That's the way it's used.

Carruthers: Please explain reserves very
slowly.

Scroggs: Reserves is an entry in the 'in'
column. It merely states where some
of the money came from: that part of
the money which has been retained in
the business. It does not state what
the money has been used for. Some
of it has gone to increase fixed assets
– the packing machine for Bill. And
some of it can go into working capital
– the extra strip metal and the
overtime for Harry and George. And
some of it can be put by for a rainy
day. You can invest it.

Carruthers: Or stash it in a bank vault.

Scroggs: If you're very sophisticated, yes.

Carruthers: Let's see if I've got this
right. Once the business has got
going, there are three places you can
get money from: your own – **share**

capital; borrowing – **loan capital**; and retained profit – **reserves**. And there are three places it can go to: **fixed assets, working capital** and **investments**.

Scroggs: He's got it! I think he's got it!

Now at last we can look at a real balance sheet.

Carruthers: We *can* look at a balance sheet but it will not get us very far because I do not understand the bit about current assets and current liabilities.

Scroggs: I see your problem. That bit is simply a snapshot of the working capital at a single moment in time, the merry-go-round suddenly frozen. Look. If I stop the factory working, you see that £30 of my working capital cash has been turned into strip metal. It's just as much of an asset as cash, but in a different form. So I have £30 of assets in **raw material**. Then I have stamped blanks – ten kilos of strip metal plus £10 of Harry's labour (which equals £40); pressed spoons – ten kilos of strip metal with £10 of Harry's labour and £10 of George's (£50). So that's £90 of assets in **work in progress**.

   Then there's a case of spoons packed by Bill and taken to the collection bay. That's £30 of strip, another £30 for three people's work – £60 – and the week's overheads of £50. That's £110 of assets in **finished goods**.

   Then there's £150 I'm owed for a consignment collected last week, and £100 I put in the bank yesterday. So here are my **current assets**:

raw material	£30
work in progress	£90
finished goods	£110
debtors	£150
cash at bank	£100

That makes £480. Take away two bills I haven't paid yet, for £30 and £50, which are my **current liabilities** – that's £80 I owe my creditors. So my **net working capital** at this moment is current assets of £480 less current liabilities of £80, which makes £400.

To summarise. There are only three places money can come from: **share capital**, which is put in by shareholders at their own risk; **loan capital**, which is money borrowed on a long-term basis; and **reserves**, which is profit put back into the business. So all the money is in the business.

There are only three places in business that money can go to: **fixed assets**, which are the things you mean to keep; **working capital**, which is the goods you mean to sell (the money can be in raw materials, work in progress or finished goods, in the bank or people can owe it to you – and don't forget to knock off the money you owe other people); and **investments**, which are savings for a rainy day or money put in someone else's business.

But does Carruthers now know how a business works?

Scroggs: He does not understand how business works because there is one thing I still have not told him. I will prove he does not understand by asking him whether he would accept this order. Look at it carefully.

Carruthers: This order is from Superior Snacketerias Limited. They want five consignments of teaspoons a week for eight weeks from 1 April. Instead of the normal £150 per consignment they will pay £200 to compensate for taking up the entire production capacity for the eight weeks. Well, because I am a sophisticated manager I can work this out. £50 extra a day is £250 a week. £250 extra a week for eight weeks is . . .

Scroggs: £2000.

Carruthers: An extra profit of £2000! I would accept this order.

Scroggs: You have not read the last sentence.

Carruthers: The last sentence reads 'payable in full by 30 September'. . .

This leads us on to the last of the three crucial documents for understanding business finance. We have considered the **profit and loss account**, which tells you what happened to your money in the past. That's your financial history book. We have looked at the **balance sheet**, which tells you where your money is at present. (That's your financial snapshot, a picture of the business frozen at a single moment of time.)

We will now deal with the third document, which tells you where your money will be going in the future. This is your financial crystal ball. It is called the **cash flow forecast**.

Scroggs: Let me ask you a few questions. How much will it cost you, every week, to make the spoons for Superior Snacketerias?

The cash flow forecast gives you the warning signal
in time to find bridging finance.

Carruthers: I think I can answer that. Fifty kilos of light alloy strip at £3 a kilo is £150. And £10 a day for each of the three lads is £30 a day – £150 a week. That makes £300. And £50 overheads – £350. It will cost me £350 a week.

Scroggs: How much will come in each week?

Carruthers: Well, that's £200 a consignment, for five days – £1000 a week.

Scroggs: But when will that £1000 actually come?

Carruthers: '. . . payment in full by 30 September.' It will arrive in six months' time.

Scroggs: So how do we pay the lads and pay the bills and buy the new lot of strip metal?

Carruthers: We have some money in the bank.

Scroggs: Yes, you have £1000 in the bank.

Carruthers: Fine. We'll use that.

Scroggs: Very sophisticated! So let us look at the cash flow forecast. We start week one with £1000. How much comes in that week?

Carruthers: Nothing.

Scroggs: How much goes out?

Carruthers: £350.

Scroggs: Which leaves?

Carruthers: £650.

Scroggs: So we start week two with . . .

Carruthers: £650.

Scroggs: How much cash comes in during week two?

Carruthers: Nothing.

Scroggs: How much goes out?

Carruthers: £350.

Scroggs: Which leaves?

Carruthers: £300.

Scroggs: So we start week three with £300.

Cash flow

Balance sheet for the present. Profit and loss account for the past. Cash flow forecast for the future.

Of course, you can examine cash flow in the past as well. Indeed a cash flow statement for the past twelve months will tell you some of the things that the profit and loss account conceals. If, for example, you had sold £10,000 worth of investments and bought £10,000 worth of new machinery, that would not appear at all in the profit and loss account. It does not affect your assets or your liabilities; it merely moves your assets into a different place. A statement of cash flow over the past twelve months, however, will show that cash has been taken out of investments and put into fixed assets.

Carruthers: £300.
Scroggs: How much cash comes in in
week three?
Carruthers: Nothing.
Scroggs: How much goes out?
Carruthers: £350.
Scroggs: Which leaves?
Carruthers: There is no need to go on. I
can see where all this is leading – I
am a sophisticated manager.

A simple profit projection does not show up
the crisis points where you may be unable to
pay your bills. Only the cash flow forecast
does that, and it gives you the warning signal
in time to find bridging finance from the
bank or write progress payments into the
contract. A cash flow forecast, month by
month or week by week, or even day by day is
the nearest thing to a crystal ball that you will
get from your accountant.

Scroggs: So you see, after eight weeks
you would have a cash deficit of
£1800, which means bankruptcy as a
result of accepting a profitable order.
Carruthers: I have changed my mind
about accepting the order from
Superior Snacketerias. My advice is
that we should not accept it.

Perhaps Carruthers should not accept it.
Perhaps he should negotiate weekly payments. Perhaps he should borrow some
more working capital from the bank. But
whatever he does, he's got to start from a
cash flow forecast. There's no perhaps
about that.
 If the cash stops going round you go out of
business – that's the rule of the game. In any
game there's a great deal more to success

than keeping the rules. But if you don't keep them, you're out. You may be marvellous at inspiring and organising your staff, and at winning their affection and loyalty and trust. Your product may be brilliant. But if you don't keep the financial rules the time will come when there's no cash to pay the staff at the end of the week, and that will have a serious effect on their affection and loyalty and trust.

Carruthers: I now understand business finance. I think. Apparently it is all about money. Money goes into **investments** – savings for a rainy day. It goes into **fixed assets** – things you mean to keep. And it goes into **working capital**, things you mean to sell. Working capital starts with raw materials. It then goes into labour to produce the teaspoons – the goods. It goes into overheads to pay the bills. Then it goes to the customer, who pays you more money than you put in. The money goes round again and you also have a bit of **profit**. Some of the profit goes in tax, some goes into dividends, and the rest goes towards making the business grow.

I also understand that the more you produce each week, the more profit you make on each consignment, because you share out the overheads. I even see that the less you produce each week, the less profit you make on each consignment, because it has to carry proportionately more of the overheads.

And I understand the three crucial documents. The **profit and loss account** tells me what has happened to my money in the past. The **balance sheet** tells me where my

The profit and loss account for the past, the balance sheet
for the present, the cash flow forecast for the future.

money is now. And the **cash flow forecast** tells me where it will be coming from in the future.

I am now ready to start my own business. You may be crude and ignorant, but you have money. Will you come in with me?

Scroggs: I may be crude and ignorant. But I am not stark staring sophisticated.

Golden rules

Remember the three documents which depict your business: the profit and loss account for the past, the balance sheet for the present, and the cash flow forecast for the future.

Don't let accountancy jargon prevent you from knowing your business. Learn the basic language and understand its uses.

Working capital is money at work. Learn where yours is in detail and make sure it is not lying idle.

Profitable companies can go bust if they can't pay their bills. Never confuse profitability with liquidity.

Profit is not champagne and cigars. It is a measure of growth or contraction of a business.

£50,000 into working capital
and what have I got?
A faulty digital egg-timer
that calculates parrots' biorhythms . . . !

Money invested in working capital
may produce nothing of any value.

2 The control of working capital

Working capital is the key to the profitability of every business. And the control of working capital is the heart of business management.

Money put into fixed assets and investments is the consequence of a single decision – shall we or shall we not buy this property, these shares, this machine tool? The decision may be right or wrong, but once it has been taken and the cheque has been signed, that is that.

But money put into working capital, on the money-go-round, is quite different. It is permanently under the control of the managers, and workers. And there is something else about working capital: more money invested in it does not necessarily get you more of anything. Money invested in loans or shares will earn more interest or dividends, but money invested in working capital may produce absolutely nothing at all, or at least nothing of any value. It may just be swallowed up without a trace.

The control of working capital means, in effect, **keeping the money tied up in working capital down to the absolute minimum level necessary to produce the sales and profits**. It means getting the best possible value, in terms of profitable sales, for every pound invested in working capital.

Carruthers: Twelve months ago I was a sophisticated corporate executive. Then a certain spoon manufacturer purported to explain to me how business works. As a result I gave up my sophisticated position and set up a fork-manufacturing business. I am now hounded hourly by my customers, my salesmen and my bank manager, and I am living on barbiturates, tranquillisers and ulcer pills.

Scroggs: I admit that is not very

sophisticated, but why are you
blaming me?

Carruthers: This charlatan persuaded me
that business finance is a sort of cash
merry-go-round. You start with a pile
of cash. You put in some of the cash
and get raw materials. You put in
more of the cash to pay the lads for
processing the raw materials into
finished goods. You put in more of
the cash to pay the overheads. The
customer collects the goods and
hands over his cash. And you use that
cash to start all over again.

Scroggs: I told you that because it is true.

Carruthers: It may be true in the spoon
business, but it is not true in the fork
business. In the fork business you
start with a pile of cash, and you put
in some for materials, some for
labour and some for overheads. But
no forks come out. So you borrow
more cash and you spend it on more
materials, more labour and more
overheads, on and on, until finally the
forks emerge and the customer
collects them. But do you get the
cash then? Oh no. He just leaves a
piece of paper. So you borrow even
more money at appalling interest
rates until at last he pays up and you
get some cash to put back into the
merry-go-round. But by then you're
in debt up to your eyeballs.

If you like, you can think of working capital as
all the money you would have to pay out in
your first week as a spoon manufacturer. For
a week you'd have to buy ten kilos of strip
metal every day, and at the end of the week
you'd have to pay the lads and pay the bills,
with no money coming in at all. In other
words, that's £350 out, and nothing in. That

is the initial investment in working capital. After that, you might sell a consignment every day and produce a consignment every day, and clear £400 a week. But you'd never stop having that £350 of dead money going through the factory. If we looked around the workshop after the lads had gone home on Friday evening, we'd still see it there: the strip on the shelf, the blanks in the workshop, the spoons in the packing room, the packed crates in the collection bay, the unpaid invoices in the file – £350 of working capital. It's there because of the time factor, because you have to buy your strip metal a week before you sell it as teaspoons. It's the physical, financial, visible expression of lead-time, or time-lag, or the delay factor, or whatever else you like to call it.

But suppose it took two weeks instead of one to turn the cash spent on materials, labour and overheads back into cash received from the customer? Suppose you had taken a fortnight instead of a week when you first started the business, a fortnight of buying ten kilos of strip a day and a fortnight of wages and bills before you started selling a consignment of spoons a day? Then you'd have £700 tied up in working capital, and not a penny more to show for it. And if you had taken a month you would have had £1400 tied up. And so on. A lot of people say time is money, but for the simple literal truth of the phrase there is no example to touch working capital.

Working capital, in fact, rests on the simple **time equals money** equation. If you increase the time it takes to produce sales revenue, you increase the working capital locked up in the business. If you can reduce the time, you liberate the capital for other purposes – which is what the control of working capital is all about.

But, as Carruthers pointed out, in the fork business even if you do produce the goods quickly, customers do not pay up on time.

Scroggs: You are quite right that customers do not always cough up.

Carruthers: Then why didn't you tell me that?

Scroggs: I didn't tell you because you are so sophisticated that you can only take in one idea at a time. Then you have to have a business lunch to recover. But the solution is very simple, luckily for you – *you* don't have to cough up either. It is quite true that when you make the sale, you don't always get cash at once. That's why there is a 'debtors' button. You often have to keep pressing your debtors till you get the cash. But there is also a 'creditors' button – your creditors give you supplies without your having to pay cash. So you keep the merry-go-round turning on credit till your debtors pay you and you can pay your creditors. The two balance out. In fact, if you conduct your business really craftily you can get cash back from the customer before you pay your suppliers.

Carruthers: What you are saying is that I should keep pestering my customers for money while not paying my own bills until the last possible moment.

Scroggs: That is a crude and blunt way of putting it. But then I am a crude and blunt man.

Carruthers: I should like to point out that I had an expensive education. I was taught never to get into debt and never to pester people for money.

Scroggs: It was an even more expensive education than you realise. You're still paying for it.

Carruthers: Very well. You have

explained that the 'sale' button does
not always produce cash, and that you
have to press the 'payment' button.
You have also explained that the
'credit' button can keep the
money-go-round moving for a time
without cash. And you have explained
that the two delays should balance
out. But that is only a small part of
my problem. It is not the real reason
for my ulcers, my insomnia or my
continual suppressed anxiety. The
real reason is that I have just
experienced a business disaster: my
company has become successful.

Scroggs: Yes. With sophisticated people,
success is normally disastrous.
Immediate failure cuts their losses.

Carruthers: I was so disastrously
successful that demand for my forks
doubled.

Scroggs: By an extraordinary coincidence,
the demand for spoons also doubled,
but that did not cause me any
sleepless nights. It caused me great
contentment. I took the extra orders,
borrowed more working capital, took
on more lads, ordered more strip
metal, and increased my turnover and
also my profit by 100 per cent. Why
haven't you done the same?

Carruthers: Because I have no money. I
have taken the extra orders, bought
some extra metal and taken on some
extra lads. But the bank will not allow
me one penny of extra money. So my
cheques are bouncing, my customers
are shouting, my salesmen are cursing
and my bank is foreclosing.

Bankruptcy through success? Yes, of course.
This can happen in several ways, the most
obvious being that you simply can't afford to

Success can be a disaster . . .

if you're not prepared.

finance the extra volume required to meet that 'successful' order. You almost certainly won't if you don't plan how to raise the necessary money and ensure that your financial commitments are not incurred long before the revenue from sales starts to come in. Then there is the problem of company costs – of course they are likely to rise to meet an expansion of business, but by how much? It is all too easy to gear yourself to expansion by increasing costs to a level which, in effect, makes the extra business unprofitable. And, of course, if the success is a 'one-off' order will those costs then go away? If you lease a new warehouse, increase the workforce – indeed add to the fixed costs in any way – you must realise that expenditure which goes on for 365 days a year is not likely to be beneficial if it equips you for orders you have now, but may well not duplicate in the future. Let us see how Scroggs has coped with success while Carruthers has not:

Scroggs: I buy five consignments of strip metal a week for £250. One a day at £50 each. I pay Harry and George and Bill £100 a week each – £300. My overheads come to £150 a week. Total cost of labour, materials and overheads – £700. And I sell five consignments of spoons a week at £200 each – £1000. So I clear £300 a week.

Carruthers: I too buy five consignments of strip a week for £250. I pay Ted and Jack and Gus £100 a week each. My overheads also come to £150 a week. Total also £700. And I sell five consignments of forks a week at £200 each – £1000. So I too clear £300 a week.

Scroggs: We both pay out the same amount and get in the same amount.

Why don't you borrow more from the bank, like I've done? I'm allowed to borrow up to £5000 working capital.

Carruthers: So am I. Unfortunately I have already borrowed £6000.

Scroggs: £6000! How have you managed to get through £6000 of working capital?

Carruthers: How much have you borrowed?

Scroggs: £600.

Carruthers: £600! How on earth do you manage on £600 of working capital?

Scroggs: I can show you my £600 of working capital. It is in my factory now. Look. There's the roll of light alloy strip that Harry collected this morning – £50. There's a roll of strip he stamped into blanks yesterday. That's £70 – £50 worth of light alloy and £20 worth of labour. There's a roll of strip he stamped into blanks and George pressed into spoons. That's £90 – the strip and two days' labour. There's a case of finished spoons packed by Bill. That's £110 – the strip and three days' labour. And there's a case labelled and documented and ready for collection. Strip plus four days' labour – £130. And add the week's overhead of £150 on to that, and there you are. Total – £600 tied up in working capital.

Carruthers: £600. So this is how the other half lives.

Scroggs: My business is efficient and profitable and I am not short of cash to expand production.

Carruthers: I may have run out of cash but at least I run my business decently.

Scroggs: And use ten times as much working capital as me for the same turnover.

Purchasing

Any manufacturing business has to buy the materials to manufacture with. Any retailing business has to buy goods for resale. And in an ideal stockroom, all the shelves are empty. Everything is purchased the day it is needed: no sooner does the van deliver it than the machine operator starts work on it, or the salesman puts it on the counter.

No business has ever achieved this ideal, and the trouble is that all too many buyers do not realise that it *is* the ideal. In fact, they believe the reverse – and what is worse, they find that the best way to keep everyone happy is always to carry generous stocks of every kind of raw material, piece-part, or sub-assembly product that anyone in manufacturing might ever conceivably ask for. That way they never get criticised by the production manager for keeping him waiting. All they have to do is buy more than they need of everything and keep it handy for emergencies.

What this means is that the price of avoiding the rare tiny delay in manufacturing is a massive over-investment in raw material stocks – like spending £5000 a year on fire insurance on a garden shed that cost £500 to put up.

Everybody in an organisation is responsible, in one way or another, for keeping working capital as low as possible – in other words for turning cash paid for materials, labour and overheads back into cash received from customers as fast as possible. But there are four key areas in a business where this process is most often delayed and where working capital can be allowed to build up to unnecessary levels if it is not permanently monitored and stringently controlled.

Those four key areas are:

1 purchasing
2 production
3 finished goods
4 credit control

These are the main areas where working capital tends to pile up unnecessarily: stacks of raw materials in stores, stacks of work in progress in the workshop, stacks of finished goods in the warehouse, stacks of unpaid invoices in the office. And that's how you reach one of the classic business crises – the **overtrading crisis.** Customers are clamouring for goods, which leads to your stepping up production to meet the demand, running out of money to finance expanded production (in other words running out of working capital), suppliers and landlords clamouring for payment, the bank refusing any more loans, finance houses foreclosing, bailiffs and receivers moving in – and all because your product was so successful. You just ran out of working capital.

And yet you didn't run out of working capital. It was there all the time. You just couldn't get at it. You had lots of working capital – lots of raw materials (the wrong materials), lots of work in progress (the wrong work), lots of finished goods (the wrong goods), a pile of unpaid invoices . . . stacks of working capital all tied up, locked up and dead.

These areas are hard enough to control even when everyone in the business is trying hard to control them. But there is a terrible pitfall, and it causes one of the central problems of management; the pitfall is that the people in control of these four areas can, and do, vastly increase the amount of working capital employed, and they increase it for worthy and conscientious reasons. They are often skilled, experienced, hard-working people and their motive is to keep everyone happy. The cost of keeping everyone happy, however, can ultimately destroy a company.

Carruthers: My business is based on four wonderful people. They're all from the same family – the Squirrel family. The first wonderful person is my buyer, Ted Squirrel. If anyone in the workshop wants anything, Ted's got it. No waiting. Every shape and size and weight. You name it, he's got it on the shelf. That takes care of £300. Wonderful chap, Ted. Keeps everyone happy.

    The next wonderful person is my production manager, Jack Squirrel. Always oblige anyone. He'll even take half-finished jobs off the machine for rush orders. Finishes them off a couple of weeks later, if necessary. Always has lots of finished forks along the gangway, so if Sales start screaming he can give 'em something to shut 'em up. Keeps everyone happy, Jack. That's £420 in the stamping section and £540 in the pressing section.

Production

The ideal production manager whips everything straight through the workshop and out again as fast as if it were a ticking time-bomb. Nothing is left half-machined, nothing is completed and kept in the factory. But again, all too many production managers find that this makes enemies. If Sales suddenly want an urgent unforeseen order, it is going to mean interrupting production and taking half-machined materials off the machine to put the rush job through. But that helps keep everyone happy. Until their firm goes bankrupt.

47

The cost of keeping everybody happy
can ultimately destroy a company.

My third wonderful person is my sales manager, Gus Squirrel. Looks after packing and dispatch. Terrific spare stocks of everything. It was Gus who made us expand our range from 3 kinds of forks to 176 kinds to meet every requirement. Always oblige a customer with a rush order. Breaks into crates for non-standard quantities. Wonderful chap, keeps all the customers happy. That's £660 for forks waiting to be packed, and £780 for finished consignments waiting for someone to order them. Oh yes, and overheads. Well of course it takes longer for things to go through a sophisticated system like mine: about six weeks. That's £900 overheads.

And finally there's my fourth wonderful person. My credit controller, Gladys Squirrel. Heart of gold.

Scroggs: She'll have to go.

Carruthers: What?

Scroggs: I know the heart-of-gold type. Unpaid customer accounts going back to World War One. But the suppliers' bills get paid the day they arrive.

Carruthers: She keeps everybody happy.

Scroggs: Delirious, I should think.

Carruthers: Wonderful girl, Gladys. Debtors, £2400. Total – £6000 tied up in working capital. I have a feeling you don't think my four wonderful people are so frightfully wonderful.

Scroggs: On the contrary, they fill me with wonder *and* fright. Fortunately *my* four people try to save money and keep the company in business, instead of spending it to buy easy popularity. They believe in using as little working capital as they can, and getting the money back as fast as

Finished goods

In the ideal company the goods roll straight out of the packing bay and through an empty warehouse on to the waiting delivery van. What's more, the range of goods offered for sale is kept to the minimum and they are sold in standard quantities. Your spoon factory makes just one kind of teaspoon, one kind of dessert spoon, and one kind of tablespoon. But this steady, continuous production of a limited range of goods does not please everyone. So, if you want to keep everyone happy, you offer 50 kinds of teaspoon, 50 kinds of dessert spoon, and 50 kinds of tablespoon. You break up cases in order to give customers exactly the number they want. And you make sure there are always plenty of cases of each of your 150 kinds of spoons in the warehouse to meet any order, however large and however unforeseen, as well as all the incomplete cases you broke into for customers who wanted non-standard quantities.

And remorselessly the working capital locked up in completed unsold goods builds up and up.

*So you think
you're in business?*

Credit control

In the ideal world your customers pay cash on the nail and your suppliers give you three months' credit. That means that your spoon factory with its one-week production cycle has cut working capital down to zero, or indeed is operating on negative working capital. Customers' cash builds up in the bank deposit account and earns you interest for three months before you pay the metal supplier or the rent.

But sometimes customers want credit, and sometimes suppliers want cash. And if you are too strict on payment terms, the salesmen criticise you for making their job harder, and if you are too slow in paying the suppliers the buyer starts to worry about getting his bottle of whisky at Christmas; so if you want to keep everyone happy you pay all the bills promptly as they come in, and give plenty of credit to customers.

Credit, of course, is just another name for lending money at no interest – you are in effect lending your customers the money to buy your goods. So all those invoices awaiting payment are simply locked-up money, more working capital, neutralised and sterilised till the customer's cheque is paid into the bank. Every day a bill remains unpaid is that bit more money tied up.

possible. If they didn't they'd be working for someone else. You, probably.

Take my buyer, Harry. He hates to see money lying idle on the shelves, so he doesn't buy *any* raw material until *just* before George needs it. George in production whips stuff through his workshop and out again as though it was a time bomb. Bill, the sales manager, reckons every crate in the delivery bay is a mark of shame. So he rushes them out to customers the second they're packed, and rushes the dispatch notes up to Prue. And Prue in accounts gets them off as though they were telegrams. And she's marvellous at persuading suppliers to give her an extra few weeks' credit.

Once cash has been turned into goods, all my four people hustle it through the system to turn it back into cash again. Everything moves so fast that there's only £600 in the pipeline before cash comes back from the customers to top it up again.

Carruthers: What an awful company. I would give a great deal not to have to work with people like that.

Scroggs: You are giving a great deal. You are giving £5400, your sleep, your health and your solvency.

Yes, four wonderful people and four effective ones. It may be a cliché that everyone in a company is 'on the same side' but you have to make sure that they all know what side that is. The first duty of a company is to stay in business, and that does not mean that everyone's interests are to be served at the expense of your firm's solvency. It does mean teaching all your staff exactly what is involved in the way they work, how it helps and how it hinders your prime objectives. Then, and only then, can your staff become both wonderful *and* effective.

But will a more realistic attitude by your staff have an adverse effect on your customers?

Carruthers: You're ignoring a vital point
   – I am not the only fork
   manufacturer in the world – I have to
   be competitive, at all costs.
Scroggs: You're right to say that you must
   compete – but *not* at all costs. £6000
   tied up in working capital is too great
   a cost.
Carruthers: Why is it too great a cost?
   All right, I'm using £6000 working
   capital, while you are using only
   £600. But if I wasn't the interest
   would only be a trifling 10 per cent
   and wouldn't solve any of my
   problems, so the point is irrelevant.
Scroggs: If it's irrelevant, why are you a
   gibbering wreck while I'm a fat cat?
Carruthers: Only because of my success.
Scroggs: The point is that having too
   much money tied up in working
   capital is not irrelevant. It is the heart
   of the problem. Listen. You told me
   last year you cleared £15,000.
Carruthers: Yes.
Scroggs: And this year business has
   doubled?
Carruthers: Yes.
Scroggs: Then why don't you double your
   production and clear an extra
   £15,000 this year?
Carruthers: I've told you – it would need
   another £6000 of working capital. I
   cannot lay my hands on £6000 of
   working capital. I have reached my
   borrowing limit.

Scroggs: So if you *could* lay your hands on
another £6000 you would not invest it
at a trifling 10 per cent, you would
use it to double production and make
yourself another £15,000 a year
profit.

Carruthers: . . . Yes.

Scroggs: You see, I only had £600 tied up
in working capital. When my business
doubled, I only needed another £600
to double production. With that £600
I doubled my purchases of raw
materials, took on more lads, and
worked a night shift as well as a day
shift. They produced double the
spoons and double the profits. I will
now show you how you can do the
same without borrowing another
penny from the bank.

Carruthers: Either you're about to
deceive me once again, or I shall be
glad I came here after all.

Scroggs: Those four wonderful people of
yours are actually wonderful jailers –
they are keeping all your money
locked up. But just suppose they
released half of it. Suppose Ted
started using up what's in his store
before buying new stocks. Suppose
Jack completed all the unfinished jobs
and let the stuff out of the workshop.
Suppose Gus made up his
consignments *and* sold off his spare
stocks. And suppose Gladys started
collecting all the money from the
debtors. If they could only get half
your working capital out of the
factory gates as forks and back in
through the letterbox as cash.
Imagine that!

Carruthers: It is not very sophisticated to
imagine things.

Scroggs: Look. You would save half your
working capital, £3000. Then you

could use that to double production.
Carruthers: It's like talking to a brick
wall. I explained to you that I need
£6000, and you come up with £3000.

What Carruthers still hasn't grasped is that
once he has managed to cut his working
capital by half, all that will have changed.

Scroggs: You will no longer need £6000
worth of working capital – you will
only need £3000 worth. So the
released £3000 will be enough to
double your raw material purchase,
double your staff, and work night
shifts as well as day shifts. Then you
can double the forks and double the
profits.
Carruthers: No, no, no. This is a trick.
Scroggs: It is not a trick. You do not
need £6000 in working capital. I
don't believe that you need £3000,
but you certainly don't need six. The
answer is this. All you have to do if
you want to save money is to save
time. If you want to run your factory
on half the money, all you have to do
is run it on half the time.
Carruthers: Half the time?
Scroggs: Yes.
Carruthers: Well, I know time is money.
Everyone says so. My wife told me so
yesterday at breakfast. I'm sure it's
true, but convince me.
Scroggs: I will convince you. Let's take
two imaginary people. One short,
quick, poor man and one tall, slow,
rich man. They both want to start up
in the knife-making business. Look at
the short man first. He rents a fully
equipped knife factory, paying rent
monthly in arrears. He gets a month's

Time is money.

credit for his raw materials, he takes on monthly paid staff and he pays his overheads monthly. Right. He's got no money, but he's got time – one month. So he moves before his time runs out. He stamps the strip, processes the blanks, packs the crates, sells the knives and collects the cash as fast as he can. By the end of the month he can pay all the bills, order more strip, start all over again and have a bit over as well. And he's never touched his own money.

Now look at the tall, slow man.

Carruthers: I can see what's coming . . .

Scroggs: He pays rent in advance, he pays for his materials on delivery, he pays his staff weekly. And he puts the Chipmunk family in charge. Ted Chipmunk keeps on buying more and more materials. A roll of strip spends a month on the shelf before going through to the factory. Jack Chipmunk keeps the workshop stuffed with finished and half finished jobs, and that strip then spends a month in the factory before it comes out as knives. Gus Chipmunk keeps the collection bay full of crates, so the same strip spends a month in the crate before the customer collects it. And Gladys Chipmunk doesn't type the invoices till the end of the month, and then mails them second class. It's another three months before the cash paid for the first roll of strip comes back from the customer.

So that's where all the money went. It went in time. Six months' rent. Six months' stock of materials. Six months' wages. Six months' overheads. All before a penny came back. And that delay is now built into the system. The materials bought

If you have accurate sales forecasts,
you don't have to overstock
for surprise orders that never come.

today will be on Ted's shelf for a
month. Then it will be in Jack's
workshop for a month. Then it will
be in Gus's crates for a month. Then
the customer won't pay for three
months.

And all that tall, slow, rich man has
to do to cut his working capital by
half is to cut the time by half. Get
Ted to carry the stocks for half as
long. Get Jack to keep it in his
workshop for half as long. Get Gus
to send the crates off to customers
with half the delay. Get Gladys to get
the cash back from customers in half
the time. Output will be the same.
Turnover will be the same. But he
will now need only half the old
working capital to do the same
business. That is why a certain
person can manage on £3000 of
working capital if he wants to.

Carruthers: You may think your
disguised character fooled me, but I
am too sophisticated for you. I could
see that you were talking about me.
You were hinting that if my four
wonderful people kept things for half
the time they do now, I could manage
on half the money.

Scroggs: That is what I was hinting.

Carruthers: But it's no good. My
wonderful people would not take the
risk of not keeping everyone happy.

Scroggs: You *can* keep everyone happy.

Carruthers: How?

Scroggs: Just follow two Golden Rules.
Golden Rule number one is **sales
forecasting**. If you have accurate
sales forecasts you know what stocks
you need to carry. You don't have to
overstock in preparation for surprise
orders that never come.

Carruthers: I have something to tell him.

He will never find a forecast that is
100 per cent accurate.

Scroggs: That's your forecast, is it? Is it
100 per cent accurate?

Carruthers: Yes ... no ... it is extremely
accurate.

Scroggs: Quite. No forecast is completely
accurate, but good forecasts can save
a fortune in unnecessary preparation
for the improbable.

When you think about it, the unnecessary
stacked-up working capital is like fat on the
human body. It is the result of unnecessary
surplus intake, it makes the functioning of
the whole body less efficient, and it shortens
life. In the same way, excess working capital
also represents wasteful excess intake, also
creates inefficiency and can also lead to
premature death. And the reason for it is the
same, too – if nobody knows where the next
order is coming from, for what product or in
what quantity or by what date, then all you
can do is put on a lot of fat and hope it will see
you through. And when you think about it,
nearly all those extra stocks are the consequence of uncertainty about future demand.

But modern industrial man does not need
fat, because he knows where the next order is
coming from. Or rather, he can get a very
good idea, within top and bottom limits, of
the likely volume and pattern of future
orders. What it needs is sales forecasting,
and sales forecasting is at the heart of the
control of working capital. So the first step in
the control of working capital is to produce
accurate sales forecasts, to keep them constantly under review, and to revise them
quickly as soon as change becomes apparent.
So the first of the two Golden Rules is to get
the fastest and most trustworthy sales forecasting system you can.

What do you think, Betty?
Are your customers really vegetarians
or just hard-up carnivores . . .?

Involve the relevant people in your company and have meetings.

Scroggs: Golden Rule number two is to
have **regular meetings** to see how
you can bring down the working
capital and keep it down.

These meetings will involve at least the
people responsible for buying, manufacturing, selling and payment collection.

Such meetings have a single purpose: to
work out all possible ways of shortening the
time between paying money to suppliers and
collecting it from customers.

More meetings? Yes. If the buyer alone
decides what stocks to delay buying he may
be sabotaging the production manager. If the
production manager makes a decision about
changing the manufacturing programme he
may leave the buyer with surplus stocks and
the sales manager short of goods. And so on.
When the whole team gets together they may
come up with suggestions for speeding up
the money-go-round: the home sales manager may be perfectly happy to promote a
different line in order to help run down the
excess stocks that resulted from a cancelled
export order, or the credit controller may get
the dispatch manager to get Friday's dispatch notes to the office before lunch so that
invoices can go out on Friday afternoon
instead of Monday morning.

If you follow the two Golden Rules –
accurate sales forecasts and **regular
meetings** between the people responsible
for the four key areas – you are well on the
way to getting working capital under control
and keeping it there.

Carruthers: But this means change. My
people won't like it. And I do not
want to upset my wonderful people.
Scroggs: Even when your customers are

shouting, your salesmen are cursing,
your cheques are bouncing and your
bank is foreclosing?

Carruthers: Even then, principles are
principles. I suppose you find that
disappointing.

Scroggs: On the contrary, I am delighted.
I have just started manufacturing
forks.

Golden rules

Accurate sales forecasts are essential.

Involve the relevant people in your company – and have meetings.

The control of working capital is the heart of business management.

Time is money – speed up the time your money takes to produce results.

The debit/creditor equation is vital.

Success can be disastrous – if you are not prepared.

The cost of keeping everyone happy can destroy a company – so motivate your staff to keep you in business.

The profit on a product or a business is determined by just three very simple factors – **cost**, **price** and **volume**. The complication is that each influences the other: cost affects price, price affects volume, and volume affects cost. There is no magic formula for striking the right balance, but there is a technique for giving yourself the best chance, and that technique is **costing**.

It will come as no surprise that our old friend Carruthers is deficient in this technique. Here he is, bankrupt, and being sold off at auction after his company went into receivership.

3 Cost, profit and break-even

Auctioneer: Finally, lot 74, managing director. Good condition, brain hardly used. Who's going to start us off? . . . Do I hear a hundred pounds . . . ten pounds . . . ten pence?

Scroggs: OK, ten pence. Come along, chum. You're mine.

Later, a bewildered Carruthers seeks an explanation.

Carruthers: I do not understand it. I simply do not understand it.

Scroggs: No. I suppose I just felt sorry for you, because I know all about you.

Carruthers: That is not what I do not understand. How can it happen that an intelligent, enterprising man can be declared bankrupt, when he has money in the bank and is selling his goods at a profit?

Scroggs: Quite easily.

Carruthers: What was that?

Scroggs: Tell me about it. After all, we are both in the same business.

Carruthers: But I am up-market and you are down-market.

Scroggs: I know. But then my business is booming and yours is bust.

Carruthers: Isn't it absurd? Is there no justice in business?

Scroggs: No, but there is logic. So tell me about it.

Carruthers: Very well. I had a brilliant idea – one of the greatest creative ideas of the century. Carruthers' Coupled Cutlery. Ideal for buffet lunches, family picnics and camping holidays. The knork – slices the sausage with one end, spears it with the other. The spork – fixes the strawberry on one end, scoops up the cream with the other. The spife – takes the jam with one end, spreads it with the other. The hiker's friend, the camper's companion. Carruthers' Coupled Cutlery! And what's more, the inventive brilliance was matched by the financial sophistication.

Scroggs: It wasn't.

Carruthers: It was.

Scroggs: I can't wait to hear about it.

Carruthers: Let me demonstrate. I calculated that I could sell my coupled cutlery for £200 a case. And that I could produce and sell ten cases a week – total sales revenue, £2000 a week. But I went into even more detail. I worked out that my costs would be only £1000 a week – for labour, materials and overheads. That meant £1000 a week profit on ten cases. See! Cost – £100 per case, and profit £100 per case.

Carruthers did his sums and worked out that it would cost him £1000 a week to produce ten cases of Carruthers' Coupled Cutlery. He was also sure he could sell them for £200 a case. This led him to produce a complex and sophisticated diagram.

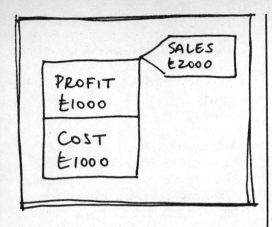

Weekly sales, costs and profit forecast (Carruthers' complex and sophisticated diagram)

Carruthers was not a man to resist or reject the findings of mathematical science. With this clear proof that he was going to make £1000 a week he went into business. And he did indeed produce cases of coupled cutlery. What is more, he sold them at £200 a case.

Scroggs: So what went wrong?
Carruthers: Nothing. It was just that I only managed to sell five crates a week instead of ten.

But of course a man like Carruthers was not going to be deterred by a little thing like that. He produced a revised diagram.

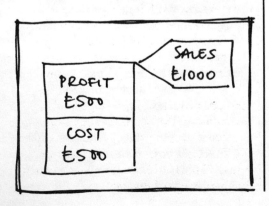

Weekly sales, costs and profit forecast (Carruthers' complex and sophisticated diagram – revised)

65

Carruthers had made the classic mistake,
and an examination of that mistake takes us
to the heart of the relationship between costs
and profits.

Carruthers: But with £100 profit per
    case, that simply meant £500 profit a
    week instead of £1000. A man can
    jog along on five hundred a week.
Scroggs: So why aren't you jogging along?
Carruthers: That is what I do not
    understand.
Scroggs: Could you show me how you
    arrived at that £1000 figure in detail?
Carruthers: You mean *even greater* detail?
    Very well. Income: ten cases at £200
    each – £2000. Expenditure: strip
    metal, ten consignments, £35 each –
    £350. Lubricants, packaging and so
    on – £50. Part-time labour, a bit of
    extra typing, a bit of help on sales –
    £100. The three lads at £100 a week
    each, £300. Overheads and general
    marketing, £200. Total expenditure –
    £1000. Subtract from income of
    £2000 . . . profit £1000. There.
    How's that?
Scroggs: Very good. Except that it didn't
    happen.
Carruthers: Well, it half happened.
Scroggs: Quite so. So would you mind
    telling me in detail what actually
    happened?
Carruthers: Why? It's bound to come out
    at £500 profit instead of £1000.
Scroggs: Even so.
Carruthers: You've got to spell it out for
    some people! All right. Income down
    to £1000 now. Half the metal – er –
    £175; half the lubricant – £25. Half
    the part-time labour – £50. Other

The working capital's threatening a go-slow, if not an all-out strike . . .

labour, well, that's three lads at £100
a week each . . .

Scroggs: Why are you still employing
three lads, with only half the turnover?

Carruthers: You can't just take on and
lay off skilled lads like mine. They'd
be off to someone else like a flash. I
have to guarantee them their jobs.

Scroggs: You mean they're staff?

Carruthers: Well, I don't eat with them,
obviously. But yes – staff. Three at
£100 – £300. And overheads still
£200.

Scroggs: So the total expenditure is?

Carruthers: . . . £750.

Scroggs: Very nice. So nice that £1000
take away £750 makes £500?

Carruthers: Precisely. What?

Scroggs: £1000 take away £750?

Carruthers: I don't understand. I'm
doing half as much business, but only
making a quarter of the profit. There
must be a mistake.

Scroggs: There's been a mistake all right.
You worked out that ten cases –
£2000 worth of sales – cost £1000 to
produce and sell and left £1000 profit.

£2000

PROFIT
LUBRICANT
STRIP METAL
LABOUR
OVERHEADS
FACTORY

£1000

PROFIT
LUBRICANT
STRIP METAL
LABOUR
OVERHEADS
FACTORY

These diagrams show what really happened to Carruthers' profits when he halved his production; they were not halved, they were quartered.

The mistake is obvious. All the same, some obvious mistakes are quite easy to make. The easiest way to make this one is to look back over the previous period when, let us say, you produced 1000 cases at a cost of £100,000, and deduce that your production costs are therefore £100 a case. Wrong – they *were* £100 a case, in the previous period. And they were only £100 *because you produced 1000 cases*. With 800 or 1200 the cost per case would have been different. So to go into a new period assuming that the cost is still £100 per case is a recipe for disaster.

Let's look at Carruthers' costs in detail.

Scroggs: So you spent £200 on overheads and marketing, £300 for the lads – that's £500. And £500 for the rest – £100 for part-time labour, £50 for lubricants and so on, and £350 for metal. But if you cut your turnover in half your overheads don't change. They are still £200. And your staff costs don't change – they are still £300. The other costs – metal, lubricants, casual labour – *do* change. They come down from £500 to £250. But it only leaves you £250 profit.

So that makes your cost per case look just a little bit different. If you're producing only five cases a week instead of ten, costs now take up three-quarters of the price of each case – £150 – and profits are only a quarter – £50.

Carruthers: But those are just accountants' figures.

Avoidable costs

These can be regarded as 'fixed', but they fall into a category that is also known as a 'policy decision' cost. The two most common are:

1 Research and development. No one says you have to do research and development, and no one will take you to court if you do not do any. But you may find that in order to stay in business you have to produce new products or improve old ones, and these costs cannot be attributed to any specific product because the product is not there yet and indeed may never be.

2 Sales and marketing. Sending a salesman out on the road is an avoidable cost, but you might be foolish to avoid it. The same could be true of advertising, exhibiting, direct mailing, market research, and all other promotional and marketing activity. And do not forget that all discounts are costs: they reduce the contribution of a sale just as much as the cost of materials or labour.

69

Research and development:
you may find that to stay in business
you have to produce new products.

Scroggs: And bank managers' figures.
    And receivers' figures. And judges'
    figures.
Carruthers: Well, what is a decent,
    honest chap supposed to do?
Scroggs: A decent, honest chap can start
    by separating his **fixed costs** from his
    variable costs. Remember we
    compared your forecast turnover of
    £2000 with your actual turnover of
    £1000? Let's look at those costs.
    Some of them didn't change – staff
    and overheads were the same, whatever
    the turnover. They're fixed costs.

Anyone who has had to deal with the real
costs of a real business will recognise the
horrifying oversimplification of Carruthers'
costings. Nevertheless some businesses –
including some successful businesses – have
been started up on the basis of back-of-an-
envelope calculations of this sort. But once
you get going you are faced with the costs of
staying in business as well as the costs of
production; and Carruthers had left out of
the record some of the latter costs as well as
all of the first. So let us take a look at some of
the main categories of fixed cost.

1 **The inevitable.** You cannot get away from
    paying certain basic fixed costs – wages,
    rent, rates, insurance, heating, lighting,
    telephone, stationery, postage and some
    basic professional fees for legal and finan-
    cial services. You may also have loan
    interest (although this may be dealt with
    separately as a finance charge).

2 **Start-up costs.** Starting up any new
    project nearly always involves special extra
    costs that do not recur once you have got
    going: making jigs, dies, and templates, for

You cannot get away from paying certain fixed costs.

example; buying equipment, furnishings and supplying promotional literature. Every business has different start-up costs, but they are always there. They will have to be paid for out of the contribution element in sales before you show any profits (with job-costing systems, these special items may be treated as a direct expense and charged to the cost of a job).

3 Selling, distribution and administration costs (these are the most frequently underestimated). Once you have customers you have selling costs, even if you have no salesmen. Orders must be taken, recorded, confirmed, dispatched and invoiced; cheques must be reconciled, entered and banked. Sales enquiries must be answered, complaints investigated, delivery errors corrected, late payers reminded, faulty goods replaced or unsatisfactory work done again. All this requires people's time and, unless you have found a way of getting it done for nothing, that means costs.

4 Depreciation. Nearly all equipment wears out. A machine costing £5000 may be worth nothing in five years' time. If so, that means its value is depreciating at the rate of £1000 a year. You are using it up as surely as you are using the metal it is pressing. That £1000 is money you are spending. Unless you record it as a depreciation cost you are fooling yourself, and you will be in for a big shock in five years' time when the machine packs up and you cannot afford to replace it.

5 Maintenance. Windows break. Roofs leak. Bulbs blow. Paint peels. Pipes leak. Drains get blocked. Machines seize up. Everyone knows these things happen, but you would be surprised how many people fail to allow for them in advance when drawing up costs.

6 Contingency. A supplier has a strike just as you are waiting for delivery to complete a contract with a time penalty clause. You can get the materials from Germany, but it means a higher price and air freight charges. Or a customer goes bankrupt while owing you a lot of money. Or . . . They will not all happen, but it is extremely foolish to assume that none of them will.

This is a very brief list of the major categories of fixed costs which even the smallest business will incur and must take into account when evaluating any new project. Scroggs develops the theme of fixed and variable costs.

Scroggs: There are, of course, costs which only arose when you produced cutlery – metal and lubricants and so on. These are the *variable* costs: £500 on ten cases, £250 on five – £50 a case. So your variable costs are £50 a case.

Carruthers: Fascinating. You are telling me that I make £150 profit on each case.

Scroggs: That is not what I am telling you.

Carruthers: What are you telling me?

Scroggs: I am telling you that we are now in a position to look for the missing figure.

Carruthers: What missing figure?

Scroggs: The key figure for any new project. The one figure you have to know before you start.

Carruthers: Which is?

Scroggs: The break-even figure. Look,

you worked out that ten cases gave you £1000 profit. Now what was the maximum you could produce a week?

Carruthers: Sixteen. Top whack.

Scroggs: But how many do you have to sell just to stay in business?

Carruthers: Nine? One? Five?

Scroggs: I don't know. Not yet. But we're in a position to work it out. We know each case has a variable cost of £50.

Carruthers: And £150 profit.

Scroggs: Not £150. How can it be profit if you haven't paid the rent or the wages or your heating bills? What about fixed costs?

Carruthers: Ah . . .

Scroggs: That £150 that's left after you've paid the variable costs is a contribution towards the fixed costs. Once you've paid those, it's a contribution to profit. At the moment all we know is that it's £150 contribution. It's the value you and your lads have added to the raw materials that you bought, by turning them into cutlery.

Your fixed costs were £500, remember? Well, you can think of them as a hole £500 deep. Each case makes £150 contribution to filling it. So two cases pay off £300 of the fixed cost. Three pay off £450. And with the four cases, you pay off the last £50 and make £100 profit. If you make a fifth case that week, then that case's £150 contribution is indeed profit – all of it.

So your break-even point in that example is 3.3 cases a week.

Carruthers: You see? I knew it! 3.3 cases a week – I was producing five! I was making a profit. Excuse me, I must go, I'm a success!!!

Scroggs: Wait a minute! I said, 'in that

That'll be £10.50, thank you, squire – think of it as a contribution to fixed costs and you won't feel so bad about it . . .

example'. But there was something I left out of that example.

Carruthers: Why?

Scroggs: Because there are some minds that cannot take in more than one idea at a time. If that.

Carruthers: What have we left out?

Scroggs: Depreciation of fixed assets.

Carruthers: Ah, of course.

Scroggs: You understand depreciation? How would you describe it?

Carruthers: Er . . . I'm not awfully good at the describing lark. But I'd be awfully interested to see how you make out.

Scroggs: Thank you. Tell me, how much did you pay for all your machines – cutters, dies, presses and so on?

Carruthers: £20,000. The whole of Aunt Agatha's legacy.

Scroggs: And how long until you have to replace them?

Carruthers: Ages. Ages.

Scroggs: How long?

Carruthers: A good five years.

Scroggs: And then you go out of business?

Carruthers: No. Then I buy some more.

Scroggs: What with?

Carruthers: Profits?

Scroggs: Suppose they're not enough? Suppose you spent them on something else?

Carruthers: All right. Tell me.

Scroggs: Right. 'Depreciation'. You started with Aunt Agatha's legacy – £20,000. And you turned it into machine tools. But it was still worth £20,000 – you just put it into machines instead of the bank. But as you use a machine, you start to use it up, just as if you were spending the money. Each case of cutlery takes a tiny bit of the machine's value with it,

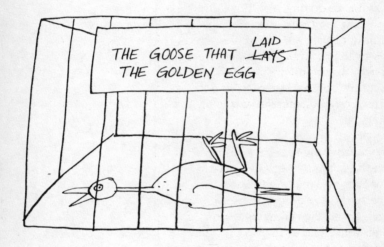

Allow for depreciation in your costings.

as well as the strip metal. It's another cost of production.

And after five years the machine's whole value will have gone. Carruthers will have spent the whole machine. So part of his sales income has to be set against that invisible expenditure of the machine's value. That's depreciation. It may look like money in the bank, but in five years' time he's going to need all of it to replace his machines and stay in business. Using up £20,000 over five years means using up £4000 a year.

And Carruthers will have to allow another £1000 a year for rising prices, because those machines won't· still cost £20,000 in five years' time. That means setting aside a total of £100 a week for depreciation.

Scroggs: You've got to be realistic. That hole isn't £500 deep, it's £600. Which means that £100 contribution from the fourth case isn't profit after all. It's swallowed up by depreciation. So your break-even point is four cases, not 3.3. Their contribution has to pay for the £200 overheads, £300 labour and £100 depreciation. So that's £600 of fixed costs and four contributions of £150 each.

Carruthers: So my break-even point is four cases.

Scroggs: So it seems.

Carruthers: Then what is all this bankruptcy charade in aid of? I was turning out five cases. I'm laughing. Aren't I?

Scroggs: Apparently not. Could there be anything you've forgotten?

Carruthers: No.

Scroggs: Tell me how you started this fascinating business.

Carruthers: Ah, what a story! All my own
idea. Got a die-maker. Prototype,
market tests, re-design. Wonderful
publicity campaign, ads, mailshots,
the lot. Launched at a buffet lunch
served exclusively with Carruthers'
Coupled Cutlery. Triumph, triumph.

Scroggs: When was all this?

Carruthers: Just over a year ago.

Scroggs: How much did it all cost?

Carruthers: Well, you don't spoil the ship
for a ha'porth of tar . . . £25,000.

Scroggs: And where did that come from?

Carruthers: Oh, that was perfectly all
right. I got a loan.

Scroggs: Interest rate?

Carruthers: 20 per cent.

Scroggs: Security?

Carruthers: Machines, patents, trade
marks.

Scroggs: Repayable when?

Carruthers: Just over twelve months.

Scroggs: And how much has been repaid?

Carruthers: . . . Nothing.

So what should Carruthers have done? He
should have carried out a proper costing,
which in this case would have been to use
marginal costing.

What is marginal costing? To put it
technically, it is the cost of producing one
more unit at the margin of your output. To
put it simply, think of a house with four
people living in it. Rent, rates, food, fuel,
insurance and general wear-and-tear come
to £100 a week – £25 a head. So what is the
extra cost if a fifth person comes to stay in the
house? Obviously not another £25 – rent,
rates and insurance do not go up at all. Fuel
and wear-and-tear go up a little, but not
much. Food goes up quite a lot. You might
find that with a fifth person, the cost of
running the house went up from £100 a week

Total absorption
costing

Total absorption costing has its
limitations. For one thing, if you
have a wide range of diverse
products, it can make it hard to
separate the more profitable from
the less profitable. For another
thing, it loads head-office rent,
bank interest and the chairman's
salary on to product costs; and, if
you are organised to give cost and
profit responsibility to subordinate
managers, you are charging them
with expenditure they have not
incurred and are powerless to
reduce. But for continuous
production of a single product
under a unitary management
structure, total absorption costing
can work perfectly well. If you use
it you do not have to worry about
calculating contribution, since all
fixed costs are absorbed into the
total figure.

to £115 a week. So the marginal cost of having a fifth person to live in the house is £15 a week.

Scroggs: You should have produced a business plan, based on a break-even figure worked out in advance.

Carruthers: You mean like you've just been doing?

Scroggs: Yes. Or there is another way. **Total absorption costing.**

Carruthers: Please, please don't confuse me with information.

Scroggs: It's simple, really. Look, how much would it cost you to produce one case a week?

Carruthers: Ah, I can do that. Fixed costs – £1200. Variable costs – £50. So that's £1250.

Scroggs: And if you produced two cases, what would they cost each?

Carruthers: Simple. Half £1250, which is, er . . .

Scroggs: What about the variable costs on the second case?

Carruthers: As I was saying. Half £1300 which is, er, £650.

Scroggs: Three cases?

Carruthers: A third of £1300 – I mean, – £1350 er . . .

Scroggs: Four cases? Five cases?

Carruthers: Hang on, hang on, old chap.

Scroggs: It's all right, I've done it for you. Five cases cost £290 each to produce. Six come down to £250. Eight come down to £200 each. And if you get up to sixteen, they're only costing you £125 each.

Carruthers: Ah, £75 contribution per case.

Scroggs: No. £75 profit. The £125 has absorbed all your fixed costs already.

Carruthers: So it has! £75 profit. Good

You can even plot the figures on a graph, with costs per unit at the side, and the number of units produced along the bottom.

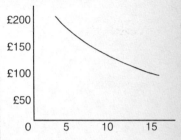

Expressed like this, you can look along the cost line and see that if you charge £150 per case, you will need to produce and sell five cases a week to break even. Or you can look up the units line and see that if you produce ten units you will need to sell them at £100 each to break even.

Lord. But where does all this get me?

Scroggs: Well, suppose you can sell ten
cases a week. Each case will cost you
£170 a case to make a profit. If you
charge less, you're in the red. Or you
can do it the other way. If you reckon
that £200 a case is the most you can
charge you can work out how many
you've got to produce to break even.
If you produce less, you're in the red.

You remember that in the case of the house
with four people living in it the marginal cost
of a fifth person staying in it was £15 a week,
since the overall running cost went up from
£100 a week to £115 a week. If you used **total
absorption costing**, you would say that the
effect of a fifth person staying in it was £15 a
week, since the overall running cost went up
from £100 a week to £115 a week. So the
effect of this fifth person coming to stay was
to lower the unit cost from £25 a week to £23
a week. You would reach this figure by taking
£100 a week shared between four people
(£25 a week each) and changing it to £115 a
week shared between five people (£23 each a
week).

Carruthers: But if I'd done one of your
costings and found out that I had to
sell eight cases a week this whole
magnificent enterprise would never
have started. I knew I couldn't
guarantee that.

Scroggs: Yes, a business plan does stop
people from starting up doomed
projects. But it also gives you a
chance to look at the alternatives.
Could you have cut your variable
costs?

Carruthers: No.

Scroggs: Used less labour?

Carruthers: No.

Scroggs: Charged more per case?

Carruthers: Not a hope.

Scroggs: Charged less per case?

Carruthers: Brilliant! The man is a commercial genius. Business brain of the century. You're going bankrupt, you must cut your profits.

Scroggs: How many cases would you sell at £150 each?

Carruthers: I'd *sell* a lot.

Scroggs: How many?

Carruthers: Fifteen a week at least.

Scroggs: What would each one cost you if you were making fifteen?

Carruthers: Er ... £130 ... wait a minute, that's £20 contribution, I mean profit per case!

Scroggs: Right!

Carruthers: £300 profit per week! I'm rich!

Scroggs: No you're not, you're bankrupt.

Carruthers: I am a retrospective millionaire.

Scroggs: The bankruptcy courts are full of retrospective millionaires.

Carruthers: But my idea works.

Scroggs: If you're right about selling fifteen cases at £150 each. And if you can actually produce fifteen cases a week. And if you can still keep your fixed costs at £1200. And if you can ...

Carruthers: Forget the trivialities. I was on to a good thing all along.

Scroggs: You may have been on to a good thing at £150 a case. It seems you were on to a bad thing at £200 a case.

Carruthers: But now I know all about it ...

Scroggs: Do you know all about it? Tell me.

Profit

The profit of a business is its revenue minus its costs. Revenue is fairly straightforward; costs, as we have seen, are not. Nevertheless, when you have paid them all, what you have left is profit.

We have already discussed profit in Chapter One. But there is one particular point to note in the relationship between profit and costs, and it is brought out most clearly by this graph.

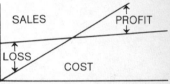

It is important because of the misleading nature of the phrase 'profit margin', which suggests that the profit on a product is in constant ratio to its price, like the margin down the side of an exercise book which stays at two centimetres whatever the length of the page. The graph shows that in fact the profit margin increases with every unit sold after break-even, or, conversely, that losses increase with every unit by which production or sales fall short of break-even.

Consequently, you can never know in advance what will be the profit margin on any given unit of production – you have to wait until the end of the year to find out what it was.

Carruthers: All right, I will. First,
marginal costing. You divide your
production costs into two different
kinds. **Fixed costs**, the ones you
have to pay whatever happens, and
variable costs, the ones you only pay
when you produce something. The
difference between the variable cost
of the product and the price you
charge for it is the contribution to
fixed costs, until they're all paid off.
When they are, that's your
break-even figure. After that, they're
contribution to profit.

Secondly, there's **total absorption
costing**. That way, you take the total
costs, fixed and variable, and divide
them by all the different numbers you
might sell. That enables you to work
out a different 'unit cost' figure for all
the different volumes.

Scroggs: Very good indeed. Twelve
months too late, but very good all the
same. And now if you'll excuse
me . . .

Carruthers: Where are you going?

Scroggs: Oh, I've got a little business to
sort out. A cutlery business. Lent
them £25,000 a year ago. Good
security – machines, patents, trade
marks – and now they've gone bust.

Carruthers: Really? Why?

Scroggs: Never worked their costs out,
never had a business plan.
Overpriced their product, and that
was that.

Carruthers: Ha! Ha! Never worked their
costs out . . .

Golden rules

Distinguish between fixed and variable costs.

Do not confuse a profit with a contribution to costs.

Know your break-even figures for each order.

Allow for depreciation in your costings.

Produce a business plan – and use it.

Carruthers seems to have made it, finally! He is now sitting behind a huge antique desk with a fat cigar and some brandy. A chart on the wall behind him shows sales over several lean years, followed by the current year's sales, which are shooting up, almost off the graph.

4
Budgeting

Secretary: There's a Mr Ron Scroggs to see you.

Carruthers: Oh yes, send him in.

Scroggs: Hello, Julian, my old mate. I thought I'd drop in as I was in the area, visiting my old Granny.

Carruthers: Your old Granny? Tell me, how is her egg-sucking technique these days? Give her a few pointers, did you?

Scroggs: There's no need to have a go at me just because I have taught you everything you know. Your problem is that so far I haven't taught you everything *I* know.

Carruthers: There is one thing you don't know. This year, entirely by my own efforts, my enterprise has taken wing. I admit we've had a few lean years, but in the first six months of this year our sales have boomed. In fact, our sales are 50 per cent higher than last year. Way beyond the target forecast. Look at the chart – and we're not even at the end of the year yet. I don't want to boast, but this could be the year of the Rolls-Royce.

Scroggs: It's that bad, is it?

Carruthers: I don't know what you're talking about. I now realise that *you* don't know what you're talking about either. Can't you understand? Sales are up!

Scroggs: Yes – up 50 per cent. Were you expecting that?

Carruthers: No, I wasn't. However, I am
    delighted that it has happened.

Scroggs: This means trouble.

Carruthers: What?

Scroggs: Don't you realise that an
    unexpected 50 per cent rise in sales
    can make just as much trouble as an
    unexpected 50 per cent fall in sales,
    or a rise in the cost of labour or new
    materials or rent or tax . . .

Carruthers: So success should be
    avoided at all costs because it's so
    disastrous, is that it?

Scroggs: Look, your sales are certainly
    accelerating, but that doesn't mean to
    say your profits are going up as well.
    Can I have a look at your budget?

Carruthers: What an extraordinary
    question.

Scroggs: You do have a budget, do you?

Carruthers: Well, the wife's got one.
    Nasty little yellow thing, keeps falling
    off its perch.

Scroggs: No. Bud-get.

Carruthers: Sorry, I thought you said
    canary. Budget, yes – it's round here
    somewhere. I remember, I put it in
    the fridge.

Carruthers takes out his budget from behind
the champagne bottles in the fridge. It is last
year's budget with 'This year plus 5 per cent'
scrawled across it.

It's obvious that Carruthers does not think
about his budget very often. But you must
have plans to run a successful business –
long-term strategic marketing ones, short-
term sales and production ones, and so on.
The most important plan of all is your
budget. It tells you where you're going and
how you're going to get there. It gives you a

destination – a target profit – and maps out a route. Other financial documents such as the balance sheet or the profit and loss account look backwards, tell you where you've been and how you got to where you are now. But you can't drive a car by looking out of the back window, and the budget gives you that vital forward view.

Most companies prepare their master budget once every twelve months – a comprehensive plan integrating all the activities, all the costs and revenues, and summarising the target profit for the year ahead. This master budget will be based on a series of mini-budgets, one for each department, according to how the company chooses to carve itself up for budgeting purposes. Whatever the pattern of 'budget centres', all must interlock together to produce the overall picture.

A budget is not a forecast. A forecast is simply an opinion, however well calculated or considered, as to what might happen. The sun might shine tomorrow, British Leyland might sell a million motor cars next year. Both of these are forecasts. A budget, even though it will be based on forecasts and on very sophisticated assumptions and guesses, is a **commitment**. When you make a budget, you commit yourself to a plan or standard of performance upon which lots of other commitments depend. If you budget to sell a million motor cars next year, then you have to commit everything in your organisation to achieving that level of performance. If you can't make that commitment, then you should revise it to something you think you can achieve – and then make a plan you *can* commit yourself to. Otherwise you risk going bust. Which brings us back to Julian Carruthers . . .

Alternative technology is one thing, Mr Bobbins
– alternative sales forecasting is another . . .

Scroggs: This is it, is it? I see you've just slapped 5 per cent on last year's budget. Now, why do you suppose you're so far out on your sales target?

Carruthers: So far *above* our sales target, you mean? Well, I admit I see this as something of a success story. Let me explain. I came up with an absolutely brilliant idea. Cutcrox Co-ordinated Cutlery and Crockery. The square-meal soup set. A square soup-plate and a square spoon. Now, you can't eat soup out of a square soup-plate with a round spoon, and vice versa. So they have to sell as a set, and sell they did.

In fact, to meet the enormous demand, Production are all working overtime – and without a murmur.

Scroggs: I'll bet.

Carruthers: Of course, it's our marketing chaps who are the real heroes. They've been running a massive press and radio advertising campaign, and the response has been, well – frankly, fantastic. In fact, Distribution have had to rent an extra van to cope with the deliveries. So, thanks to our enormous sales our profits are going to be fantastic.

Scroggs: Your sales may well be up 50 per cent, but I very much doubt if your profits will be.

Carruthers: No, our profits will be up 250 per cent!

Scroggs: What?

Carruthers: Let me make it easy for you. Last year our income was £100,000. Of that, £20,000 was profit. This year sales are up 50 per cent, that's £150,000. So profit is going to be £70,000, up by £50,000. You see?

Compared with last year's £20,000 that's up by 250 per cent.

Scroggs: And this is all quite different from your original budget?

Carruthers: Oh yes. This all came as a very pleasant surprise.

Scroggs: Well, you're half right. It is a surprise.

Carruthers: You mean it's not pleasant?

Scroggs: Let's find out. Last year your income was £20,000 above expenditure. But this year, according to your budget at least, expenditure is going to rise by 5 per cent.

Carruthers: But don't forget that, according to my budget, income was going to rise by 5 per cent too. So it's still well ahead of expenditure.

Scroggs: But it didn't happen that way, did it?

Carruthers: No, of course it didn't. Income went up and up and up.

Scroggs: How did it go up so fast?

Carruthers: Sales.

Scroggs: Look – you've been pouring out money to achieve those sales. And in pouring it out you've been increasing your expenditure. How much did your massive advertising campaign cost you?

Carruthers: Oh, that – £40,000. Well, maybe I'm not doing as well as I thought. But I'm still in profit.

Scroggs: Yes, but how much did all that extra overtime cost?

Carruthers: Only about £30,000.

Scroggs: And how about your distribution costs? Renting an extra van, sending stock out by rail?

Carruthers: Yes . . .

Scroggs: How much?

Carruthers: . . . £20,000.

Scroggs: So your costs have shot up by £90,000 and your income has only

gone up by £50,000. Now do you
see? You're in way over your head.
What you're looking at now is not a
50 per cent profit, it's a loss. You're
not waving, you're drowning.

Carruthers: How was I supposed to know
that that was happening?

Scroggs: By using your budget.

A budget isn't something you just compile
and then file. Once you've prepared a
budget, however good or bad, you don't put it
in the fridge to stop it going off. You use it to
manage the business, or your part of it. Any
budget is only as good as the work you put in
to **create** it in the first place, and then what
you do to **monitor** and **control** it. You must
consult it regularly and take corrective action
where needed to keep on course.

What went wrong for Carruthers – the
basic budget mistake – is that he never
looked at his budget from one year to the
next. It's no good just slapping an across-
the-board increase on last year's figures to
arrive at this year's figures. And the idea is
not to wait until the end of the year to look at
this year's budget and see whether you've
'beaten' it. Remember, budgeting is about
looking forwards, not backwards. About
planning for the wine you will buy to
celebrate the end of the year, not waiting
until 31 December to see whether you want
to drown your sorrows or paint the office red.

Carruthers is totally surprised by a 'boom'
in his sales over the last year, and interprets
this as good fortune without stopping to
explore the consequent effects throughout
his business. A 50 per cent increase in sales
revenue doesn't mean an automatic increase
in profit, and he spends an extra £40,000 on
advertising, £30,000 on overtime and
£20,000 on extra distribution, without any
check on whether he can really afford to. He

thinks he's going to be swimming in champagne but he might in fact be drowning in a rather stormy sea.

Scroggs: Your budget is the most precise tool you've got for measuring your company's performance. So use it. Look, your departments have been spending every penny that came from sales and now they're spending money that isn't even there.

Carruthers: Good point. But how will my budget help?

Scroggs: A budget shows you where you're going. Of course your sales chart is important, but that only shows you where you've been. You can't set out on a journey and only look backwards. Better still, plot a course, and that's what your budget should be.

Carruthers: So my budget is my course through the future, is it?

Scroggs: Yes, although yours is not a very good one, is it? I mean, if you were planning a five-mile journey, and you ended up fifty miles away, I'd say you'd plotted a pretty rotten course, wouldn't you?

Carruthers: Well, room for improvement certainly.

When you prepare a budget, you work out all the sources of revenue and all the areas of costs; decide what you think you can sell, for how much, and what it will cost you to do so. But what other people think is as important as what you think and it can't be over-emphasised that good budgeting is as much about the proper handling of **people** as it is about the proper handling of **money**. Anyone who is preparing a budget must consult his colleagues, his subordinates and his superiors. These people must be involved, to help decide what yardsticks should be used, and whether a proposed budget is realistically feasible. It is important that other people should participate in the standard-setting process for two main reasons. First, it helps you set more realistic standards. Second, it makes it much harder for people to complain at a later stage if the plan doesn't work out and they have to alter things. Involvement from the start will increase motivation and help boost morale if the going gets rough. In a similar vein, budgeting is a vital part of delegation. If you give people discretion to make their own decisions to achieve agreed goals, then performance against budget is a good method of assessment.

Scroggs: Tell me, Julian, how did you construct your budget?

Carruthers: Easy. I cast an eye over last year's figures and saw they were about 5 per cent up across the board on the previous year, so I carefully slapped on another 5 per cent and Bob's your uncle – this year's budget.

Scroggs: But you were 50 per cent out on sales, and 250 per cent out on profit and loss, so you say.

Carruthers: Yes, but what you're not taking into account is . . . tell me about budgets.

Scroggs: Right. What do you need to make a budget?

Carruthers: Luck?

Scroggs: Judgement.

Carruthers: I see. Of course. I use my judgement.

Scroggs: Wrong. You use everybody's judgement. Take advantage of your staff's knowledge, experience and

Participation in budget preparation
makes it harder for people to complain later
if the plan doesn't work out and they have to alter things.

judgement to assess the factors that are likely to influence the company's performance. Why don't we go back to the beginning of the year and make your budget all over again?

Carruthers: Very well, if you think it will help.

Scroggs: Right. These are the things you've got to do with a budget. You construct it. You make the best guess of the year's income and expenditure. Then you coordinate it. Check that each department's plans mesh in with each other's and don't conflict with them. And then you use it to control business, month by month all through the year. Now let's take these one at a time. First?

Carruthers: Construct.

Scroggs: Right. Now, you construct your budget by considering income, expenditure and profit. So what are you going to aim for?

Carruthers: Easy. Income – one billion pounds, expenditure – nil, profit – one billion.

Scroggs: No. That's unrealistic.

Carruthers: It's very attractive.

Scroggs: But you have to consider reality.

Carruthers: All right. Er . . . how about 6 per cent on last year's budget . . . 7 per cent? All right – 27 per cent. No, no – 492.31 per cent.

Scroggs: Look, you can't create your budget on your own. You need the knowledge and judgement of the people who are going to be creating the income and expenditure and profit. So, to construct your budget you first of all consult your departments – to keep it simple let's say Production, Marketing and Distribution. You need their estimates of performance, their

Budget centres

Companies segment themselves in many and wondrous ways. Carruthers, simple soul that he is, goes for three main divisions or budget centres: **Production**, who make the square-meal soup sets; **Marketing**, who sell them and **Distribution**, who deliver them.

Each of these divisions will incur costs in order to meet the sales. A distinction has to be made between 'fixed' costs (expenses which can't be avoided whatever happens – such as factory and office rent and rates) and 'variable' costs (which can be more quickly adjusted – such as advertising expenses, overtime payments, material purchases and the like).

Each division has to count its costs separately, in as much detail as is practicable and possible. Production must calculate how much raw material it will have to buy to produce the budgeted volume, how much it will spend on wages, how much on machinery. Marketing will incur expenditure on salaries and cars, and also on advertising and promotion. Distribution too will have salaries, plus packaging, petrol, insurance, maintenance.

mini-budgets to help you create your master budget.

The sales forecast gives the revenue target. What did Carruthers do when he was preparing his new sales forecast? 'Easy. I cast an eye over last year's figures, saw they were about 5 per cent up across the board, so I carefully slapped on another 5 per cent and Bob's your uncle – this year's budget.'

Using as much market intelligence as possible, Carruthers should have looked at the size of the market last year, considered anything likely to alter the size of it this year, found out what the competition were up to, sought out any changes in social habits or dining behaviour likely to affect his product sales and so on. Above all, he should have talked to his sales force. What do they think they can sell?

There will be guesswork and assumptions, but since you will be stuck with the figures you decide upon, you should aim to be as realistic as possible. If Carruthers had more than one product, say knives, forks and spoons, his sales forecast would necessarily become more complex – taking into account not only the quantities of each product to be sold, but also the mix between different products and their relative prices.

Scroggs: So, you'd better start with your expected sales. Why not consult your marketing department?

(Carruthers picks up the telephone and calls Marketing.)

Carruthers: Hello? Carruthers here. Tell me, how many cases can you sell a day?

There will be guesswork and assumptions,
but you should aim to be as realistic as possible.

Marketing manager: Well, if we carry on
with present sales schedules I reckon
we could shift fifty, sixty, seventy . . .
oh no, let's call it sixty. We can
definitely shift sixty cases a day.

Carruthers: Sixty cases a day at £10 per
case! We're looking at £600 per day
income here. Hooray! Now . . .

(He dials the production department.)

Carruthers: Production? Do you think
you could come up with sixty a day
for us?

Production manager: Eighty.

Carruthers: Pardon?

Production manager: Well, me and the
lads could knock out eighty cases a
day – no danger.

Carruthers: Eighty? My word, at £10 per
case that's £800 income . . .

(Dazed, Carruthers dials another number.)

Carruthers: Could your distribution
chaps handle eighty cases a day?

Distribution manager: Eighty? A
hundred more like.

Carruthers: One hundred? That's £1000
a day. This is wonderful.

Carruthers is now heading for worse trouble
than ever. It is pointless for each division
within a company to calculate its own budget,
and then have them all lumped together.
Budgets have to fit together, which demands
coordination.

You have to start with your **major
limiting factor**, which for many companies
is likely to be 'how many can we sell?' For
others, it might be 'how many can we make?'
or there could be other constraints which
impose a natural limit on the business.

Having decided what the limiting factor is, you can gear everything else to suit.

The **cash budget** will always be an important variable too. This plans the availability and flow of money, lets you know what you can afford and when. In most larger companies, this will be the province of the management accountants, but it will play an important role in the coordination process. Cash, too, could therefore be a limiting factor.

Let's take a closer look at how, under tuition, Julian Carruthers managed to co-ordinate his budget.

Carruthers: *Scroggs!* We can distribute a hundred cases a day – that's £1000.

Scroggs: You can only make eighty.

Carruthers: True . . . but that's still £800 a day.

Scroggs: You can only sell sixty.

Carruthers: Only sell sixty . . .

Scroggs: And that is what we call a limiting factor. In this case the limiting factor is how many cases can you sell? Answer, sixty cases a day.

Carruthers: Still, £600 a day. That's not bad, is it?

Scroggs: You tell me. How much will it cost you?

Carruthers: Let's have a think. For a start there's overheads – about £50 a day, and next there's production – at a rough guess . . .

Scroggs: Don't make a rough guess. Find out.

(Carruthers rings the production department.)

Carruthers: It's me again. How much would you say it would cost to produce these sixty cases a day?

Production manager: Like I said, we

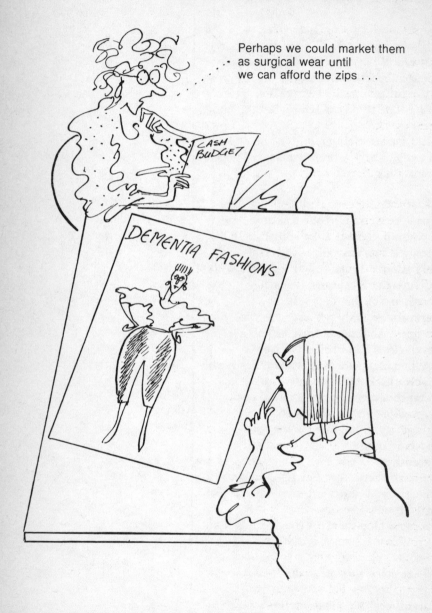

The cash budget plans the availability and flow of money.

could do more. But for sixty it would cost us £250 a day.

Carruthers: Not bad. Now . . .

(He rings the marketing department.)

Carruthers: What would it cost you to cope with sixty cases a day?

Marketing manager: For sixty cases a day – a mere £250.

Carruthers: Only £250? Good, good. Now for Distribution . . .

(He telephones Distribution.)

Distribution manager: £150 a day – that's all it would cost.

Carruthers: Excellent, excellent. Well, look at this, Scroggs – £250 a day and £250 a day and £150 a day plus £50 for the overheads, that's all it costs.

Scroggs: And added together?

Carruthers: Added together – £700 a day.

Scroggs: To produce sixty cases at £10 each, making . . .

Carruthers: Now wait a minute. There's something very wrong here.

Scroggs: No, so far you've done everything right, you've constructed your budget.

Carruthers: But it says I'm going to make a loss.

Scroggs: So what do you do?

Carruthers: Coordinate?

Scroggs: Go on, then. Coordinate.

Carruthers: I'd absolutely love to, but I don't know what it means.

Scroggs: It means that you adjust each department's expenditure budget in the light of the others', and of the overall income budget, until they all fit together into a workable plan that

Alternative standards

The budgeting process generates standards which have to be met throughout the company. It's important to distinguish three different types of standards.

Ideal standards have people and machines working flat out and never making mistakes or breaking down. Such standards are likely to prove unrealistic, too high and can easily demotivate. **Past standards** follow custom and practice – what's always been done. Whilst people tend to feel comfortable with these, they are likely to contain errors, inefficiencies and anomalies. **Currently attainable standards** allow people to have the odd cup of tea, and for things to go wrong occasionally, but still get a high enough standard to motivate and achieve a good end result.

Zero-based budgeting can be a useful technique too. This is the notion that you don't start your budget assumptions from what you did last year, but from scratch. This will allow you to get rid of inefficiencies which have crept in over the years, and can be helpful in cutting out 'slack' or 'padding' in budgets.

leaves you a decent profit. Why not call a meeting?

Carruthers: Good idea.

Later . . .

Marketing manager: Excuse me, Mr Carruthers, but I was just thinking – shoot me down in flames if I'm wrong here – but I reckon we could shift 120 cases a day if we went into an intensive radio and press advertising campaign.

Carruthers: 120, eh? £1200 a day! Production?

Production manager: 200.

Carruthers: Pardon?

Production manager: If you can get us an extra machine press and if the lads work overtime, you're looking at 200 cases a day.

Carruthers: £2000!

Distribution manager: We can't handle that.

Carruthers: You can't?

Distribution manager: I told you – 100 cases a day, top whack. But of course, if we had another van, we could deliver 250 a day.

Carruthers: £2500!

Scroggs: It'll cost you.

Carruthers: Yes, but I can work that out. Limiting factor – sales of 120 cases a day, that's £1200 a day. Now, that's against overheads at £50 a day, then there's production at £250 a day, plus leasing a new machine press at £150 a day, plus overtime at £50 a day. Next – marketing at £250 a day plus press advertising at £50 a day, plus radio advertising at £200 a day. Finally – distribution at £150 a day, plus extra transport at £150 a day. So we've got income £1200,

The budgeting process generates standards
which have to be met throughout the company.

expenditure . . .

Scroggs: £1300.

Carruthers: Oh crumbs – we're still running at a loss.

Distribution manager: Excuse me, but remember I told you we could deliver 100 cases a day if we were without the extra van.

Carruthers: 100 cases? Well, how about Marketing? What would it cost you to sell 100 cases?

Marketing manager: Well, we could still move 100 cases if we forgot the radio advertising and just went for the press advertising.

Carruthers: And Production?

Production manager: We could produce 100 without a new machine, but the lads would still have to work overtime.

Carruthers: So, to produce 100 cases a day at £10 each – namely £1000 income – it would cost £50 a day overheads, £250 a day production plus only £50 for overtime as we won't be needing the extra machine. Add on £250 a day marketing, plus only £50 for press advertising as we're not going for radio. And finally – distribution – £150 plus nothing because distribution say they can deliver 100 cases a day in the first place, so that's an income of £1000 against an expenditure of £800 – that's £200 profit!

Scroggs: Mr Carruthers, I'm very impressed. Are you happy?

Carruthers: I'm modestly exuberant, I can tell you that.

Scroggs: What about everyone else?

Carruthers: Well, I can tell them that, too.

Scroggs: No, no. Are they satisfied with your plans? Don't forget they have to

commit themselves to your budget if
it's going to work.

Carruthers: Commit themselves? Oh
yes . . .

Scroggs: You won't get the best out of
them if they're not satisfied that the
budget's sensible. Constructing a
budget isn't just about handling
figures, it's about handling **people**
too. So when you've constructed the
budget, made your best guess and
then coordinated it so everyone
agrees about the future pattern of
performance, you can move on to the
last stage. Where are you going?

Carruthers: I'm going to put the budget
in the fridge. I don't want it to go off.

Scroggs: But it's a tool, remember?
You've still got to use it – that's the
last stage.

Carruthers: How? No, don't tell me . . .

Scroggs: Control.

There's no guarantee that everything will
work out according to plan. But once agreed,
to, **the master budget must be adhered to**
– not as a straitjacket, but as a decision-
making tool. If you've done the job properly
and created an accurate budget, your goal
must be to stick to it, however hard to bear it
may sometimes seem.

If you don't do this you risk damaging the
company. 'Beating' the sales budget, for
example, can give nasty shocks to Production
and Distribution if they can't keep up, or
can't keep up at an economical cost. Could
the sales budget have been more accurate to
start with? Or, if you generate surplus cash,
you may take the finance director by surprise
and simply land the company with higher tax
bills. Of course, it's better to beat a budget
than to be beaten by it, but the best thing is to
be spot on.

Beating the sales budget can give nasty shocks
to Production and Distribution if they can't keep up.

So **performance must be monitored.** 'How are we doing?' 'Are we getting to where we said we would?' These are key questions to be asked if the budget, and the business, is to be controlled.

Carruthers: So how do I control my budget?

Scroggs: Well, are you just going to turn out 100 cases every day for the whole year?

Carruthers: No. We'll sell more at Christmas and June.

Scroggs: June?

Carruthers: Wedding presents for the June brides, bless 'em. And February and August are slack months.

Scroggs: And costs?

Carruthers: Definitely.

Scroggs: How will that affect costs?

Carruthers: Oh, you mean bigger sales in June mean bigger marketing and distribution costs in April and bigger production costs in March. That sort of thing?

Scroggs: Exactly. So why not go back to the beginning of this year and work out costs department by department and month by month.

Carruthers: And sales?

Scroggs: And sales. Right. It's January again.

Carruthers: Happy old year!

Scroggs: We'll see about that. Now, you've **constructed** your budget, **coordinated** your budget and you've got **commitment** to your budget. Now you have to **control** the budget month by month.

Carruthers: Right. January sales budget – £20,000.

Scroggs: Actual?

Carruthers: Spot on.

Scroggs: Costs?
Carruthers: Overheads – £1000,
    production – £6000, marketing –
    £6000, distribution – £3000. That's
    £16,000.
Scroggs: Actual?
Carruthers: Spot on again.
Scroggs: Very good. Variance?
Carruthers: No thanks, never touch them
    . . . what's a variance?
Scroggs: The difference between
    budgeted performance and actual
    performance.

The frequency with which a manager should
monitor his or her budget and check for
variances will vary, often according to his or
her level within the organisation. To compare just three different levels, for example:
the production supervisor or salesperson on
the road might check his or her performance
daily, the production or sales manager might
check weekly, and the director on the board
might monitor monthly.

The key determinant is: how quickly do
you need to know about variances in order to
be able to do something about them?

Having discovered a variance you must ask
what caused it. Have we lost orders? Have we
spent too much on raw materials, or used
more materials than we thought we would to
achieve a given level of output – a variance on
the 'yield'? Have we spent too little or too
much on promotion? The nature of the
variances will clearly differ according to the
nature of the company and the budget. The
vital point is to know about them, with
sufficient time and information to do something about them.

Watch out too for variances which arise
through bad timing rather than bad budgeting. In other words, you may overspend in
March because you had to incur costs which

you had expected to come through in April. But this will sort itself out by the beginning of May. This type of 'phasing' variance can occur particularly in sales. If you have a booming month, be careful to check that it's not caused by orders which you would have had anyway, simply brought forward. Otherwise you might have a nasty hole later in the year, which you hadn't allowed for.

Scroggs: So. Nil variance for January. February?

Carruthers: Er . . . sales budget – £18,000. Actual – £20,000. Success! I told you.

Scroggs: Costs?

Carruthers: Well – budget at £16,000, actual costs – £17,000.

Scroggs: Why?

Carruthers: Production was up a bit.

Scroggs: Variance?

Carruthers: Well – sales up £2000, costs up £1000. Variance – £1000.

Scroggs: Positive variance – £1000. Now, March. Costs?

Carruthers: Budget – £18,000. Actual – £21,000. I told Production that they could lease that extra machine after all.

Scroggs: Sales?

Carruthers: Down £2000. Costs up £3000. Er, variance – £5000.

Scroggs: Negative variance. Running variance?

Carruthers: What?

Scroggs: Well, it's obvious, isn't it? You had no variance in January, and gained £1000 in February. So your running, or cumulative, variance was positive to the tune of £1000. In March you dropped £5000 against budget, so at the end of March your running variance is £5000 negative

plus of course the February surplus –
so that makes £4000 negative. Now,
April?

Carruthers: Sales up £1000. Costs up
£5000. (Distribution – extra
transport.) Negative variance –
£4000. Running variance – £8000.

Scroggs: May?

Carruthers: Sales £2000 down. Oh
no . . . costs £8000 up – the TV
campaign. Negative variance –
£10,000. Running variance –
£18,000.

Scroggs: Negative.

Carruthers: All right, all right.

Scroggs: June?

Carruthers: Ah, the June brides. Sales
down £7000? They must have been
slimming. Costs up £1000 – there
was a rent review.

Scroggs: Negative variance – £8000.
Running negative variance – £26,000.
£2000 loss instead of a £24,000
profit. There goes the Rolls-Royce.

Carruthers: I see what you mean. What
can I do?

Scroggs: Control. Losing control means
you must **review, react** and **revise**.
First **review**.

Carruthers: We've done that.

Scroggs: Well, **react**.

(Carruthers bursts into tears.)

Scroggs: That's reasonable. But we must
also do something.

Carruthers: Do you mean reduce costs?
Cut back on advertising, sell the new
van, postpone re-equipment?

Scroggs: Or increase sales. Boost
advertising in the most promising
region. Or try a price cut, or an
export drive. You see, there are
positive ways of getting the business

back on course as well as negative ways. But what matters is to react in time.

But in reacting to variance in the budget managers can't just sigh or smile. They have to react or report to everyone else who needs to know. Since every element in a budget has consequences for every other – if it's been properly coordinated – it's very important to keep people in the know. For example, a production variance could occur if a machine failed. If this were likely to cause prolonged problems, Production should let Marketing know. Otherwise Marketing might commit the company to orders which can't be met, or spend money unwittingly advertising products it can't deliver.

Don't just react to the news of someone else's variance with, 'Oh, what rotten luck.' What does this mean for your bit of the business? What corrective action needs taking? If you lose a big order you were expecting, don't just sit and moan. You either need to find a replacement order, or revise all the budgets accordingly.

Scroggs: Finally, at the last stage, **revise** your budget.
Carruthers: You mean change the budgeted expenditure from July up to December?
Scroggs: And the budgeted income. In other words, change all the figures you now realise are going to be wrong.

Don't compile then file. **Monitor continuously**. Then take control action as appropriate either to get the budget back on to its original budget commitments or to take account of the new facts.

Although the management accountant can draw attention to variances when they occur, it's down to the managers responsible to take the necessary action – and above all, to decide which action to take.

Much will depend on how significant the variance is. Remember that variances can go either way, too much or too little, positive or negative. A favourable variance can cause just as many problems as an unfavourable one, if it's a significant amount. In every case, action will be needed. Should we increase advertising expenditure to boost sales? Should we increase production to meet sales figures higher than budgeted? Should Marketing be cut back because Production can't keep up? Should the whole budget be revised to meet the new position?

Carruthers: You mean I should do another budget?

Scroggs: He's got it! By George, he's got it.

Carruthers: Still, that will take some working out. Hold on . . .

Scroggs: Yes?

Carruthers: I could have another get-together with the lads. Consult, create and coordinate and then use the new budget to control again.

Scroggs: At last!

Carruthers: Now I understand budgets. The budget is the company's course through the future created by the company. **Construct**, **coordinate**, **control**, and to control your budget you've got to **review**, **react** and **revise**. I also now understand that my buoyant sales chart may not be quite the good news I thought it was. However, there is still hope.

Five 'don'ts'

Don't just add X per cent to last year's figures to arrive at this year's. The entire circumstances may have changed, and past performance is just one guide among several.

Don't indulge in wishful thinking of the 'we sold 100 this year, but only 80 last, so we'll sell 120 next year' variety. The vital question is, what evidence is there? You need more to go on than faith.

Don't be deliberately pessimistic, either because you're lazy and want an easy time, or because you like to be able to show off later and say, 'Look, I beat my budget!'

Don't deliberately pad your budget, generating unnecessary expenditure this year because you fear future cut-backs.

Don't use budgets as political weapons for building empires, taking on excess staff or resources simply to promote the status and importance of your own department.

Scroggs: Indeed there is. Until the next time?

Carruthers: Thank you, Scroggs. By the way, how are things with you? Ticking over all right?

Scroggs: Mustn't grumble. Branched out, actually. Entirely new line.

Carruthers: Really, what are you selling now, then?

Scroggs: Business training manuals. Cheerio, squire.

Golden rules

A budget is a tool – not an ornament.

A budget is only as good as the work put in to create it in the first place.

Prepare your budgets in consultation with others. Construct, coordinate, control.

A budget is not a forecast, it is a commitment.

Compare your 'actuals' against your budget regularly, and examine the variances.

Never be afraid to re-budget as circumstances change. Review, react, revise.

Other
Video Arts books
published by
Methuen

So you think you can manage?

Managers often find themselves confronting situations of considerable complexity – which is all the more reason why the principles of management itself should be simple, easily grasped and helpful in dealing with those situations. Too often, poorly equipped managers allow the opposite to happen; their approach to management gets in the way of what they are supposed to be managing. Such bosses are a menace and should be suppressed. In this book you will find many examples of these people. But you will also follow them as they learn the ropes, get down to it, improve; and in following them, you will improve as well.

So you think you can manage? combines wit and wisdom as it takes the would-be manager through how to organize himself and others, taking decisions, writing letters, chairing meetings, conducting interviews and the overall skills of management.

This first book of a spectacular new series follows the style and approach of the Video Arts training films, introducing us through scenes and dialogue to the failings of managers and the problems confronting them before moving on to the remedies. Key points are summarised and highlighted, and a list of Golden Rules is given at the end of each chapter.

So you think you can sell?

Selling is the key to business – selling goods, services and ideas. The good salesperson is essential to any company and, if you are involved in selling, improving your performance could earn you a golden future.

So you think you can sell? is the unique Video Arts combination of wit and wisdom, comedy and common sense which takes you along the road to successful selling. It introduces you to the basics – knowing your product, knowing its benefits, knowing your customer and establishing a relationship in which a sale will result. It examines the pitfalls – too much jargon, concentrating on what you have to say rather than what the customer wants to hear – and takes you through the techniques of the 'cold call', telephone sales, the proposal, the demonstration, the negotiation, and many other aspects of selling. And it describes how to deal with the many types of potential client who fall into the category of 'awkward customers' – the suspicious, the hostile, the ditherer, the know-all, the silent.

If you want to improve your selling skills, this book will be invaluable. If you think you have nothing to learn, it will be even more so.

After **So you think you can manage?** this is the second book in a new series following the style and approach of the Video Arts training films, introducing the reader through scenes and dialogue to the failings of salespeople and the problems confronting them before moving on to the remedies. Key points are summarised and highlighted, and a list of Golden Rules is given at the end of each chapter.

Leabharlann Caisleán Átha Cliath